POEMS OF TO-DAY

Third Series

THE ENGLISH ASSOCIATION

(FOUNDED 1906)

President 1946 : ARTHUR BRYANT
Chairman of Committee : ARUNDELL ESDAILE, Litt.D.

AIMS AND ACTIVITIES

1. To unite and introduce to one another those who are interested in English Language and Literature, whether as writers, teachers, artists, actors, or administrators ; and to act as a link between groups engaged in specialized English work.

2. To uphold the standards of English writing and speech ; to contribute to English letters, scholarship, and research ; to discuss methods of English teaching ; and to encourage especially the work of younger members.

3. To spread as widely as possible the knowledge and enjoyment of English Literature.

4. To put these aims into practice by providing lectures, readings, discussions, social functions, a magazine and other publications ; and to organize occasional visits to dramatic performances and places of literary interest.

5. Literary Advice Panel (for detailed particulars please apply to the Secretary).

SUBSCRIPTIONS

(*a*) The financial year runs from January 1 to December 31, and a subscription paid at any time during the year entitles a member to the magazine "ENGLISH" (three numbers) and the Presidential Address.

(*b*) The annual subscription to the Central Body is 10*s*. 6*d*., or with *Essays and Studies* and *The Year's Work in English Studies* (post free), £1 1*s*., and is due in January.

Life Membership (which does not cover *Essays and Studies* and *The Year's Work in English Studies*) is £7 10*s*. Life Membership subscription can be compounded on the basis of a deduction of 1*s*. 6*d*. for every annual subscription paid.

(*c*) The annual subscription of a full member of a Branch is fixed within certain limits by the Branch, and is usually 7*s*. 6*d*., or with *Essays and Studies* and *The Year's Work in English Studies* (post free), 18*s*.

(*d*) Subscriptions to the Central Body should be made out in favour of the English Association and sent to Barclays Bank Ltd., 95 Victoria Street, Westminster, S.W.1. Further information will be given to intending members, or they will be placed in communication with the Hon. Secretary of any Branch by the Secretary, 3 Cromwell Place, London, S.W.7.

POEMS OF TO-DAY

THIRD SERIES

PUBLISHED FOR THE ENGLISH ASSOCIATION
BY
MACMILLAN AND CO., LIMITED
ST. MARTIN'S STREET, LONDON
1946

First Edition 1938
Reprinted 1943, 1945, 1946

PRINTED IN GREAT BRITAIN
BY R. & R. CLARK, LIMITED, EDINBURGH

PREFATORY NOTE

IN this anthology the intention which prompted the First and Second Series of *Poems of To-day* is continued. Its aim is to bring together a selection of contemporary poetry representative of a span of years, and at the same time sufficiently in accordance with tradition to avoid excursions into the fields of ultra-modernism.

Beginning where the Second Series concluded, the following collection consists of poems published since 1922 down to the present day. The period has been characterized by a large body of verse in which the traditional modes of the poetic art have been challenged or disregarded. No attempt has been made to represent the more extreme forms of this movement. On the other hand the book will be found to include a number of poems that are truly typical of the modern school, while yet conforming to certain accepted canons of style. The omission of the more extravagant manifestations of modern poetry implies no judgment on it, but is dictated by the deliberate intention to preserve continuity with the character of the preceding books. A preference for traditional technique is perhaps justified by the tendency, already apparent among poets, to return to older forms and patterns.

Rather more verse of a light quality is included than before, as an antidote to that poetry of disillusionment which is a necessary feature of the anthology if it is to be really representative of its period. Some verse also of which the chief distinction is its musical quality has been admitted as a relief from the dissonance so often audible in the poetry of social and intellectual revolt.

Although no effort has been spared to make the selection fully representative it is regretted that it has not been possible to obtain permission to include examples of the work of some poets whose names are well known.

January 1938

INDEX OF AUTHORS

INDEX OF AUTHORS

INDEX OF AUTHORS

INDEX OF AUTHORS

INDEX OF AUTHORS

INDEX OF AUTHORS

INDEX OF AUTHORS

ACKNOWLEDGMENTS

For permission to use copyright poems, the English Association is greatly indebted to the authors; to the literary Executors of Julian Bell (Mr. Quentin Bell), Robert Bridges (Mrs. Bridges), John Drinkwater (Miss Winifred Gwyn Jeffreys), John Freeman (Mrs. Freeman), Thomas Hardy (Miss Irene Cooper Willis), Gerard Manley Hopkins (Mr. Gerard Hopkins), D. H. Lawrence (Mrs. Lawrence), Harold Monro (Mrs. Monro), Wilfred Owen (Mrs. Owen), and Geoffrey Scott (Miss Iris Origo); and to the following Publishers in respect of the poems enumerated:

Messrs. Ernest Benn & Co., Ltd.
A. P. Herbert, *My Ship* (No. 68).
Messrs. Boriswood, Ltd.
Rex Warner, *Poems* (Nos. 147, 148, 149).
Cambridge University Press, The
F. L. Lucas, *Poems* (Nos. 80, 81, 82, 83).
Messrs. Jonathan Cape, Ltd.
Lilian Bowes Lyon, *Poems* (Nos. 22, 23).
W. H. Davies, *Poems* (Nos. 33, 34, 35).
Michael Roberts, *Poems* (Nos. 117, 118, 119, 120).
Andrew Young, *Poems* (Nos. 159, 160, 161).
Messrs. Chatto & Windus.
Richard Eberhart, *The Groundhog* (No. 49).
Wilfred Owen, *Poems* (Nos. 101, 102, 103, 104).
Frederic Prokosch, *Poems* (Nos. 110, 111).

ACKNOWLEDGMENTS

MESSRS. R. COBDEN-SANDERSON, LTD.
Edmund Blunden, *Poems* (Nos. 16, 17, 18).
Harold Monro, *Poems* (Nos. 94, 95).

MESSRS. CONSTABLE & CO., LTD.
Walter De La Mare, *Poems* (Nos. 42, 43, 44).
Robin Flower, *Personality* (No. 50).

CRESSET PRESS, THE
Ruth Pitter, *Poems* (Nos. 108, 109).

MESSRS. J. M. DENT & SONS, LTD.
Clifford Dyment, *Poems* (Nos. 46, 47, 48).
Edwin Muir, *Poems* (Nos. 96, 97, 98).
Herbert E. Palmer, *Poems* (Nos. 105, 106, 107).
W. J. Turner, *Nostalgia* (No. 145).

NOEL DOUGLAS
Hilton Brown, *To a Panther* (No. 26).

MESSRS. GERALD DUCKWORTH & CO.
Edith Sitwell, *Poems* (Nos. 126, 127, 128, 129).
Osbert Sitwell, *Poems* (Nos. 130, 131).

MESSRS. FABER & FABER, LTD.
W. H. Auden, *Poems* (Nos. 3, 4, 5, 8).
George Barker, *Poems* (Nos. 10, 11, 12, 13).
Roy Campbell, *Poems* (Nos. 27, 28, 29).
Charles Madge, *Poems* (Nos. 88, 89, 90).
Herbert Read, *Poems* (Nos. 113, 114, 115).
Stephen Spender, *Poems* (Nos. 132, 133, 134, 135, 136).

MESSRS. HAMISH HAMILTON,, LTD.
L. A. G. Strong, *The Mad-Woman* (No. 137).

MESSRS. WILLIAM HEINEMANN, LTD.
John Masefield, *Wood-Pigeons*, (No. 91).
Siegfried Sassoon, *Poems* (Nos. 122, 123).
Laurence Whistler, *The Glass Chandelier* (No. 151).

ACKNOWLEDGMENTS

HOGARTH PRESS, THE

Cecil Day Lewis, *Poems* (Nos. 36, 37, 38, 39, 40, 41).

JOHN LEHMANN, *This Excellent Machine* (No. 79).

MESSRS. HERBERT JENKINS, LTD.

Guy Boas, *Doubt* (No. 21).

LANE (JOHN), THE BODLEY HEAD, LIMITED

Louis MacNeice, *Iceland* (No. 86).

John Pudney, *The Moonbathers* (No. 112).

MESSRS. LAWRENCE & WISHART, LTD.

W. H. Auden, *Poems* (Nos. 6, 7).

MESSRS. MACMILLAN & CO., LTD.

Wilfrid Gibson, *Out of the Air* (No. 56).

Thomas Hardy, *Poems* (Nos. 60, 61, 62).

Phyllis Hartnoll, *The Dancer, and Other Poems* (Nos. 63, 64).

Christopher Hassall, *Poems of Two Years* (Nos. 65, 66, 67).

Sean O'Casey, *Within the Gates* (Nos. 99, 100).

Dorothy Wellesley, *Poems of Ten Years* (No. 150).

W. B. Yeats, *Collected Poems* (Nos. 153, 154, 155, 156, 157, 158)

MESSRS. MATHEWS (ELKIN) & MARROT, LTD.

G. M. Cookson, *Poems* (Nos. 30, 31).

MESSRS. METHUEN & CO., LTD.

A. S. J. Tessimond, *Poems* (Nos. 141, 142).

MESSRS. JOHN MURRAY

Lord Gorell, *The Coat* (No. 57).

ACKNOWLEDGMENTS

OXFORD UNIVERSITY PRESS, THE

Robert Bridges, *Cheddar Pinks* (No. 25).

Gerard Manley Hopkins, *Poems* (Nos. 69, 70, 71, 72, 73).

E. H. W. Meyerstein, *A Sundial* (No. 93).

Geoffrey Scott, *Poems* (Nos. 124, 125).

Jan Struther, *Poems* (Nos. 138, 139).

POETRY BOOKSHOP, THE

Frances Cornford, *A Glimpse* (No. 32).

RICHARDS PRESS, LTD., THE

John Gawsworth, Poems (Nos. 53, 54).

MESSRS. SECKER (MARTIN) & WARBURG, LTD.

Lascelles Abercrombie, *The Stream's Song* (No. 1).

D. H. Lawrence, *Poems*, (Nos. 75, 76, 77, 78).

SEIZIN PRESS, THE

James Reeves, *The Hour and the Storm* (No. 116).

MESSRS. SIDGWICK & JACKSON, LTD.

John Drinkwater, *Who were before Me* (No. 45).

The Editors of the following publications courteously confirmed the permissions given by the authors: *English* in respect of No. 2 by J. Redwood Anderson; of No. 15 by Laurence Binyon; of No. 55 by Wilfrid Gibson; of No. 59 by I. Sutherland Groom; of No. 93 by E. H. W. Meyerstein; of No. 146 by James Walker, and of No. 152 by Humbert Wolfe. *The Listener* in respect of Nos. 7 and 9 by W. H. Auden; of No. 87 by Louis MacNeice; of No. 88 by Charles Madge; of No. 92 by Huw Menai, and of No. 143 by Dylan Thomas. *The London Mercury* in respect of No. 10 by George Barker; of No. 24 by A. C. Boyd; of No. 51 by John Freeman, and of No. 150 by Dorothy

Wellesley. *Punch* in respect of No. 19 by Cicely Boas; of No. 20 by Guy Boas; of No. 26 by Hilton Brown; of No. 58 by C. L. Graves; of No. 74 by E. V. Knox, and of No. 140 by Dorothy Margaret Stuart. *The Spectator* in respect of No. 120 by Michael Roberts.

The Association desires also to thank authors and publishers for their generosity in waiving and reducing customary copyright fees, in view of the special objects which the Association exists to promote.

BIOGRAPHICAL NOTES

ABERCROMBIE, LASCELLES (1881–1943). Born in Cheshire. Educated at Victoria University, Manchester. Professor of English Literature, University of Leeds, University of London (Bedford College), and Goldsmiths' Reader in English, Oxford University. His published works include—*Interludes and Poems*; *Mary and the Bramble*; *The Sale of St. Thomas*; *Emblems of Love*; *The Theory of Poetry*; *Romanticism*; *Collected Poems*, and *Poetry: Its Music and Meaning*.

ANDERSON, J. REDWOOD (1883). Born at Manchester. Educated at home, and for a short period at Trinity College, Oxford. Assistant Master at Hymers College, Hull, 1915. His published works include—*Flemish Tales*; *Walls and Hedges*; *Haunted Islands*; *Babel*; *The Vortex*; and *Transvaluations*. Has contributed to *Chapbook*; *To-Day*; and various Anthologies.

AUDEN, WYSTAN HUGH (1907). Born at York. Educated at Gresham's School, Holt, and Christ Church, Oxford. King's Gold Medal for Poetry, 1936. His published works include—*The Dance of Death*. Has contributed to various periodicals.

BARKER, GEORGE (1913). Educated at Marlborough Road School, Chelsea. His published works include—*Alanna Autumnal*; *Poems*; *Janus*, and *Calamiterror*.

BELL, JULIAN (1908–1937). Born in London. Educated at Leighton Park, and King's College, Cambridge. Professor of English Literature, Wuhan University, 1935–1936. Killed while driving an ambulance on the Madrid front. His published works include—*Winter Movement*; and poems in *Cambridge Poetry*. Edited *We did not Fight*.

BINYON, LAURENCE (1869–1943), C.H. Born at Lancaster. Educated at St Paul's School, and Trinity College, Oxford. Newdigate Prizeman. Keeper of Prints and Drawings at the British Museum; Charles Eliot Norton Professor of Poetry, Harvard University. His published works include—*Paris and Oenone*, *Attila*, *Arthur* (plays); *Lyrical Poems*; *Odes*; *Blake*; *Catalogue of English Drawings in the British Museum*; *Poetry and Modern Life*; *The Sirens*; *Landscape in English Painting and Poetry*, and *Painting in the Far East*.

BIOGRAPHICAL NOTES

BLUNDEN, EDMUND CHARLES (1896). Educated at Cleave's Grammar School, Yalding, Christ's Hospital, and Queen's College, Oxford. Served in the War in France and Belgium. Awarded Hawthornden Prize, 1922, and Benson Medal of the Royal Society of Literature, 1930. Professor of English Literature at Tokyo University, 1924–1927; Fellow and Tutor in English Literature, Merton College, Oxford, since 1931. His published works include—*The Waggoner and Other Poems*; *The Shepherd and Other Poems of Peace and War*; *To Nature*; *Undertones of War*; *Poems*, and *The Face of England*.

BOAS, CICELY (1898). Author of *The Vicar's Wife* and *A Farmer's Marriage*: contributor to *Punch* and *The London Mercury*.

BOAS, GUY (1896). Educated at Radley College, and Christ Church, Oxford. Senior English Master, St. Paul's School; Headmaster of Sloane School, Chelsea; "G. B." of *Punch*. His published works include—*Lays of Learning*; *Traffic and Theatre Rhymes*. Editor of *An English Book of Light Verse*; *A Punch Anthology*, etc. General Editor of *The Scholar's Library* Associate Editor of *English*.

BOWES LYON, LILIAN (1895). Born at Beltingham, Northumberland, was for a short time a home-student at Oxford, but did not read for a degree; can milk and plough, and has travelled a little. Her published works include—*The Buried Stream*; *The White Hare*, and *Bright Feather Fading*.

BOYD, A. C. (1902). Educated at Moira House, Eastbourne, and University College, London. Librarian. Has contributed verse and prose to *The Adelphi*; *English*; *London Mercury*; *New Verse*; *Sunday Referee*; *The Poet's Vision*, and *The Year's Poetry*, 1937.

BRIDGES, ROBERT SEYMOUR (1844 – 1930). Born in Kent. Educated at Eton, and Corpus Christi College, Oxford. Qualified in Medicine. Poet Laureate, 1913. His published works consist of poems and plays, and critical essays, and include—*Milton's Prosody*; *Poetical Works*; *Britannia Victrix*; *October*; *New Verse*. His last work, *The Testament of Beauty*, has been very widely read and highly praised.

BROWN, HILTON (1890). Born in Elgin. Educated at Elgin Academy, and St. Andrews University. Entered Civil Service. His published works include—*Dictators Limited*; *Ostrich Eyes* (Novels); *The Second Lustre*; *Both Sides of Suez*; *Potter's Clay*; *Maya* (Short Stories). Has contributed to *Punch* over initials H. B., *Blackwood's Magazine*, and *Cornhill Magazine*.

CAMPBELL, ROY DUNNACHIE (1902). Born at Durban, Natal. Educated at Durban High School, and Natal University.

Played wing three-quarter for Natal University. Took three cocardes in the Arena at Arles and Nîmes, 1921. Won the cocarde at the grand taurine gala of Istres, November 11, 1931, fighting and throwing the bull single-handed without the aid of cape. Member of the Toro Club and of La Joyeuse Lance. His published works include—*The Flaming Terrapin*; *The Wayzgoose*; *Adamastor*; *The Georgiad*; *Flowering Reeds*, and *Broken Record*.

COOKSON, GEOFFREY MONTAGUE (1867). Born at Dallington, Northampton. Educated at Clifton, and Balliol College, Oxford. Ceylon Civil Service. His published works include—*Denys of Auxerre* (a lyrical drama); *A Verse Translation of Aeschylus*; also of *Faust*, Part I (Routledge Broadway Translations); *Poems* 1932.

CORNFORD, FRANCES (1886). Born at Cambridge. Grandfather was Charles Darwin, and her mother was Ellen Wordsworth Crofts, lecturer at Newnham College. Educated privately. Her published works include—*Poems*; *Spring Morning*; *Different Days*, and *Mountain Path*.

DAVIES, WILLIAM HENRY (1871–1940). Born at Newport, Monmouthshire. Was apprenticed to a picture-frame maker, and became a tramp in America. Returned to England and led a penurious life in London lodging-houses and as a pedlar in the country. His published works include—*The Autobiography of a Super-Tramp*; *A Poet's Pilgrimage*; *Collected Poems*; *Forty New Poems*; *Song of Life*; *Secrets*; *The Song of Love*, and *My Birds*.

DAY LEWIS, CECIL (1904). Born in Ballintubber, Queen's Co., Ireland. Educated at Sherborne School, and Wadham College, Oxford. Master at Cheltenham College Junior School. His published works include—*Country Comets*; *Transitional Poem*; *From Feathers to Iron*; *The Magnetic Mountain*; *A Hope for Poetry*; *A Time to Dance*, and *Starting Point*. Has contributed to many Reviews.

DE LA MARE, WALTER JOHN (1873). Born in Kent. Educated at St. Paul's Cathedral Choir School, London. F.R.S.L.; Hon. Litt.D. (Cambridge). Spent eighteen years in commercial life before devoting his time to literature. Awarded a Civil List pension for the distinction of his literary work. His first volume of verse, *Songs of Childhood*, was published under the pseudonym Walter Ramal. His published works include—*Poems*; *The Return*; *The Listeners*; *Peacock Pie*; *Memoirs of a Midget*; *Come Hither* (an anthology); *Stuff and Nonsense*; *The Fleeting and Other Poems*; *Themselves when Young*; *Collected Poems* 1929 *and* 1934, and *The Wind Blows Over*.

BIOGRAPHICAL NOTES

DRINKWATER, JOHN (1882–1937). Educated at Oxford High School, was for a time in various Assurance offices. He was co-founder of The Pilgrim Players, which developed into the Birmingham Repertory Theatre Company. His best-known plays, *Abraham Lincoln* and *Oliver Cromwell*, were produced in London. His published works include—*Olton Pools*; *Seeds of Time*; *Collected Poems*; *Persephone*; *Inheritance*; *Summer Harvest*; *Shakespeare*, and *A Pageant of England's Life*.

DYMENT, CLIFFORD (1914). Born at Alfreton, Derbyshire. Educated at Loughborough Grammar School, Leicestershire. Poet, short-story writer, book reviewer, and film critic. Author of two volumes of poems: *First Day*, and *Straight or Curly?*

EBERHART, RICHARD (1904). Born in Austin, Minnesota. Educated at Dartmouth College, New Hampshire, and St. John's College, Cambridge. Tutor in the household of King Prajadhipok of Siam; Assistant Master in the English Department of St. Mark's School, Southborough, Massachusetts. His poems are included in *Cambridge Poetry*, 1929; *New Signatures*; *The Faber Book of Modern Verse*, and in various periodicals. His published works include—*A Bravery of Earth*.

FLOWER, ROBIN (1881). Born at Meanwood, Yorkshire. Educated at Leeds Grammar School, and Pembroke College, Oxford. After leaving Oxford joined the staff of the British Museum, where he is now Deputy Keeper of the Manuscripts. His published works include—*Eire*; *Hymenaea*; and a series of privately printed brochures; *Thanksgiving*; *The Leelong Flower*; *The Great Blasket*; *Monkey Music*, and *The Pilgrims' Way*. A volume of translations from the Irish, *Love's Bitter Sweet*, was printed at the Cuala Press in 1925. A collected edition, *Poems and Translations*, was published in 1931.

FREEMAN, JOHN (1880–1929). Born in London. Awarded the Hawthornden Prize, 1920. Chief Executive Officer in the Department of National Health Insurance. His published works include—*Memories of Childhood and Other Poems*; *Lyrical and Narrative Poems*; *Prince Absalom*; *Solomon and Balkis*; *Collected Poems*, and *Last Poems*.

GAWSWORTH, JOHN (T. I. Fytton Armstrong) (1912). Born in Kensington. Educated at Merchant Taylors' School. Freeman of the City of London. Founded The Twyn Barlwm Press. His published works include—*Known Signatures*; *Ten Contemporaries*, and *Edwardian Poetry*. Editor of *Full Score*; *The Poets of Eton*; *The Poets of Harrow*; *The Poets of Merchant Taylors'*, and biennially, *Neo-Georgian Poetry*, a miscellany of contemporary verse.

BIOGRAPHICAL NOTES

GIBSON, WILFRID WILSON (1878). Born in Northumberland. His published works include—*Daily Bread*; *Fires*; *Thoroughfares*; *Battle*; *Friends*; *Livelihood*; *Dramatic Reveries*; *When*; *Home*; *I heard a Sailor*; *Collected Poems*; *The Golden Room*; *Island Poems*, and *Fuel*.

GORELL, LORD (1884). O.B.E., 1918, C.B.E., 1919. Educated at Harrow, and Balliol College, Oxford. Barrister; President of Royal Society of Teachers, 1929; Chairman of the Society of Authors; Partner in John Murray (publisher); Chairman of Royal Aero Club; Editor of the *Cornhill Magazine*. His published works include—*Love Triumphant and Other Poems*; *Pilgrimage*; *Many Mansions*; *Although*; *Unheard Melodies*, and *Poems*, 1904–1936.

GRAVES, C. L. (1856–1944). Educated at Marlborough, and Christ Church, Oxford. Assistant Editor of *The Spectator*; member of the *Punch* Staff and Assistant Editor. His published works include—*Horace Odes*, *Book V*, English Versions, with Rudyard Kipling; *Mr. Punch's History of the Great War*; and numerous other volumes.

GROOM, IDA SUTHERLAND. Born in London. Educated privately, at the City of London College, and in France. Her published works include—*Partialities* (a series of Sonnets). Contributor to *English*, *The Poetry Review*, and other periodicals, *A Reciter's Repertory*, and other anthologies.

HARDY, THOMAS (1840–1928). O.M., 1910. Born in Dorset. Architect, poet, and novelist. His novels include—*Far from the Madding Crowd*; *The Return of the Native*; *The Mayor of Casterbridge*; *Tess of the D'Urbervilles*; *Jude the Obscure*; and among his volumes of poems are—*Wessex Poems*; *Time's Laughing-Stocks*; *Satires of Circumstance*; *Moments of Vision*; *Collected Poems*; *Winter Words*, and a play, *The Dynasts*.

HARTNOLL, PHYLLIS (1906). Educated at St. Hugh's College, Oxford (Scholar). Gained Newdigate Prize, 1929, for *The Sands of Egypt*. Licenciée-ès-Lettres. Her published works include—*Twenty Poems*, and *The Dancer and Other Poems*.

HASSALL, CHRISTOPHER VERNON (1912). Educated at St. Michael's College, Tenbury, Brighton College, and Wadham College, Oxford. Member of the O.U.D.S.: played Romeo. Toured Egypt and Australia in modern comedy. Played in a season at the Old Vic. His published works include—*Poems of Two Years*; *Devil's Dyke, with Compliment and Satire*, and *Christ's Cornet* (a poetic drama).

HERBERT, ALAN PATRICK (1890). Educated at Winchester (Exhibitioner) and New College, Oxford (Exhibitioner). Barrister; M.P. for Oxford University; member of the Staff of *Punch*. Introduced The Matrimonial Causes Bill, 1937. His published works include—*The Bomber Gipsy*; *The Secret Battle*; *The House-by-the-River*; *Light Articles Only*; *The Wherefore and the Why*; *Tinker, Tailor*; *The Man about Town*; *The Old Flame*; *The Blue Peter*; *Laughing Ann*; *She Shanties*; *Riverside Nights*; *Plain Jane*; *Misleading Cases*; *The Trials of Topsy*; *Topsy, M.P.*; *Honeybubble & Co.*; *La Vie Parisienne*; *The Water Gipsies*; *More Misleading Cases*; *Holy Deadlock*; *Ballads for Broadbrows*; *No Boats on the River*; and he has also written several Librettos.

HOPKINS, GERARD MANLEY (1844–1889). Born in Essex. Educated Highgate School, and Balliol College, Oxford. Entered the Roman Church, 1866; entered Jesuit Novitiate, 1868. Appointed to Chair of Greek, Royal University of Ireland, 1884. Publications—none during his lifetime. His poems, edited by Robert Bridges, were issued posthumously in 1919.

KNOX, EDMUND GEORGE VALPY (1881). Educated at Rugby, and Corpus Christi College, Oxford. Editor of *Punch*. Pen-name "Evoe." Served in the War. His published works include—*The Brazen Lyre*; *A Little Loot*; *Parodies Regained*; *These Liberties*; *Fiction as She is Wrote*; *An Hour from Victoria*; *Fancy Now*; *It Occurs to Me*; *Gorgeous Times*; *Quaint Specimens*; *Awful Occasions*; *Poems of Impudence*; *I'll tell the World*; *Wonderful Outings*; *Here's Misery*; *Blue Feathers*; *This Other Eden*; *Things that Annoy Me*; *Slight Irritations*, and *Folly Calling*. Has edited also an *Anthology of Humorous Verse*.

LAWRENCE, DAVID HERBERT (1885–1930). Born in Nottinghamshire, son of a coal miner. Educated at the Nottingham High School, and the Nottingham Day Training College. Became a teacher in an elementary school. Travelled widely. His published works include—*Love Poems and Others*; *Sons and Lovers*; *Amores*; *Poems*; *Look! We have Come Through*; *New Poems*; *Tortoises*; *Birds, Beasts, and Flowers*; *Pansies*; *Collected Poems*; *Last Poems*, and a play, *The Daughter-in-Law*.

LEHMANN, JOHN (1907). Born at Bourne End. Educated at Eton (King's Scholar), and Trinity College, Cambridge. Editor of *New Writing*, and joint-Editor of *The Year's Poetry*. His published works include—*A Garden Revisited* (poems); *The Noise of History* (poems in verse and prose), and *Prometheus and the Bolsheviks* (a travel book about the Caucasus).

LUCAS, FRANK LAURENCE (1894). Born at Hipperholme. Educated at Rugby, and Trinity College, Cambridge. Pitt

University Scholar, Porson Prizeman, Browne Medallist, Chancellor's Medallist; Fellow and Librarian of King's College, Cambridge. Served in 7th R. West Kent Regiment, and Intelligence Corps. Student of British School at Athens. Membre Correspondant Honoraire de L'Institut Littéraire et Artistique de France. His published works include—*Euripides and his Influence*; *Euripides' Medea* (translation); *Authors Dead and Living*; *Tragedy*; *The Complete Works of J. Webster*; *Eight Victorian Poets*; *Studies French and English*; *The River Flows*, *Cécile*, *The Wild Tulip* (novels); *Time and Memory*, *Marionettes*, *Ariadne* (poems); *Poems*, 1935; *From Olympus to the Styx* (with Prudence Lucas); *The Art of Dying* (with Francis Birrell); *Crabbe*, *Beddoes*, *Rossetti*, *and Tennyson* (anthologies); *Four Plays*; *The Decline and Fall of the Romantic Ideal*. and *The Golden Cockerel Greek Anthology*.

MACNEICE, LOUIS (1907). Born in Belfast. Educated at Marlborough, and Merton College, Oxford. Lecturer in Classics (University of Birmingham), and Lecturer in Greek at Bedford College for Women (University of London). His published works include—*Poems*; *The Agamemnon of Aeschylus* (translated into verse); *Out of the Picture* (a play), and *Letters from Iceland* (with W. H. Auden).

MADGE, CHARLES (1912). Born in Johannesburg. Educated at Winchester, and Magdalene College, Cambridge. Founder and organiser of "Mass-Observation" sociological group. His published works include—*The Disappearing Castle* (poems); *Mass-Observation* (with Tom Harrisson), and *May the Twelfth* (with Humphrey Jennings).

MASEFIELD, JOHN (1878), O.M., Hon. D.Litt. (Oxon). Born at Ledbury, Herefordshire. Had an adventurous youth at sea. Lived in America, 1895–1897, and earned his living by doing odd jobs. Began his career as a critic and editor of poetry in 1903. Poet Laureate in succession to Robert Bridges. His published works include volumes of poetry, novels, plays, essays, and short stories. Among them are—*The Everlasting Mercy*; *Dauber*; *The Daffodil Fields*; *Sonnets*; *Reynard the Fox*; *Enslaved*; *Right Royal*; *King Cole*; *The Dream*; *Collected Poems*; *Sard Harker*; *Odtaa*; *Midsummer Night*; *The Bird of Dawning*; *End and Beginning*; *The Taking of the Gry*, and *The Square Peg*.

MENAI, HUW. Born at Carnarvon. Was hawker, newspaper seller, messenger, and errand-boy. Went to South Wales, where he took up active Socialist propaganda, and contributed to *The Socialist Review*, and *The Social Democrat*. Became a weigher at the pit. Unemployed for some years. His published works include—*From the Upcast Shaft*; *The Passing of Guto*, and *Back in the Return*.

MEYERSTEIN, EDWARD HARRY WILLIAM (1889). Born at Hampstead. Educated at Harrow, and Magdalen College, Oxford. Assistant at the British Museum (Dept. of MSS.), served in the 3rd Bn. of the Royal Dublin Fusiliers. His published works include—*The Door*; *The Trireme*; *Wade's Boat*; *Voyage of Ass*; *The Monument*; *Grobo*; *The Pleasure Lover*; *The Boy*; *A Life of Thomas Chatterton*, and *Beauty and the Beast*.

MONRO, HAROLD (1879–1932). Born in Brussels. Educated at Radley, and Caius College, Cambridge. Founder of the *Poetry Review*, and afterwards *Poetry and Drama*, in conjunction with the Poetry Society. Founder of the Poetry Bookshop in London. His published works include—*Judas*; *Before Dawn*; *Children of Love*; *Trees*; *Strange Meetings*; *Real Property*, and *The Earth for Sale*.

MUIR, EDWIN (1887). Educated at Kirkwall Burgh School, Orkney. A clerk in various commercial and shipbuilding offices in Glasgow. His published works include—*The Marionette*; *The Three Brothers*; *First Poems*; *Chorus of the Newly Dead*; *Transition*; *Structure of the Novel*; *John Knox*; *Variations on a Time-Theme*; *Poor Tom*, and *Journeys and Places*.

O'CASEY, SEAN (1884). Born in Dublin. Dramatist. His published works include—*The Plough and the Stars*; *The Silver Tassie*; *The Shadow of a Gunman*; *Juno and the Paycock*; *Within the Gates*, and *Windfalls*.

OWEN, WILFRED (1893–1918). Killed in action in the War. A volume of his poems was published in 1920, with an introduction by Siegfried Sassoon.

PALMER, HERBERT EDWARD (1880). Born at Market Rasen. Educated at Woodhouse Grove School, Birmingham University, and Bonn University. Schoolmaster, journalist, and lecturer. His published works include—*Two Fishers*; *Songs of Salvation, Sin, and Satire*; *The Judgement of François Villon*; *The Teaching of English*; *Cinder Thursday*; *Collected Poems*; *The Roving Angler*; *Summit and Chasm*; *The Mistletoe Child: autobiography of Childhood*, and *The Vampire*.

PITTER, RUTH (1897). Born at Ilford, Essex. Educated at elementary and secondary schools. War Office, 1915–1917. Artist for Walberswick Peasant Pottery Co., in Walberswick and London, 1917–1930. Now in business in Chelsea in wholesale hand-painted goods. Her published works include —*First Poems*, 1920; *First and Second Poems*, 1927; *Persephone in Hades*; *A Mad Lady's Garland*, and *A Trophy of Arms* (awarded the Hawthornden Prize). Has contributed poems to *The New Age*.

PROKOSCH, FREDERIC (1909). Born at Madison, Wisconsin. Educated in America, Austria, England, France, and Germany, and Yale and Cambridge Universities. Teacher of English at Yale University. Has travelled most of his life. His published works include—*The Asiatics* (novel); *The Assassins* (poems), and *The Seven Who Fled* (novel). Has done considerable research work on Chaucerian MSS.

PUDNEY, JOHN (1909). Born at Langley. Educated at Gresham's School, Holt. Contributor to *Time and Tide*, *Listener*, *New Statesman*, *London Mercury*, and *Life and Letters*. His published works include—*Spring Encounter*, and *Open the Sky*.

READ, HERBERT (1893), D.S.O., M.C., Hon.D.Litt. Born at Kirbymoorside. Educated at Crossley School, Halifax, and Leeds University. Captain the Green Howards; Assistant Keeper Victoria and Albert Museum, 1922–1931; edited the *Burlington Magazine*. His published works include—*Naked Warriors*; *Reason and Romanticism*; *Collected Poems*; *English Prose Style*; *Phases of English Poetry*; *English Pottery*; *The Meaning of Art*; *Art Now*; *English Stained Glass*, and *Art and Society*.

REEVES, JAMES (1909). Born at Harrow. Educated at Stowe School, and Jesus College, Cambridge. Teacher of English in Canterbury, London, and Chichester, successively. His published works include—*The Natural Need*. He was a collaborator in *Epilogue*.

ROBERTS, MICHAEL (1902). Educated at Bournemouth School, King's College, London, and Trinity College, Cambridge. Physics Master at Royal Grammar School, Newcastle-upon-Tyne. His published works include—*These Our Matins*; *Poems*; *Critique of Poetry*, and *The Modern Mind*; edited *New Signatures*; *New Country*, and *Elizabethan Prose*. With E. R. Thomas has produced a volume of the "Classics of Scientific Method": *Newton and the Origin of Colours*.

SACKVILLE-WEST, VICTORIA (The Hon. Mrs. Harold Nicolson) (1892). Born at Sevenoaks. Her published works include—*The Land* (awarded the Hawthornden Prize, 1927); *Poems of West and East*; *Orchard and Vineyard*; *King's Daughter* (poems); *The Edwardians*; *All Passion Spent*; *Family History*; *The Dark Island* (novels), and *Pepita* (biography); *Collected Poems*, and *Some Flowers*.

SASSOON, SIEGFRIED LORAINE (1886). Educated at Marlborough, and Clare College, Cambridge. Served in the War, 1914–1918. Was Literary Editor of the *Daily Herald* in 1919. His published works include—*The Old Huntsman*; *Counter Attack*; *War Poems*; *The Heart's Journey*; *Memoirs of a Fox-Hunting Man* (awarded the Hawthornden Prize, 1929); *Memoirs of an Infantry Officer*, and *Vigils*.

SCOTT, GEOFFREY (1884–1932). Educated at Rugby, and New College, Oxford. Winner of the Newdigate Prize, and the Chancellor's Essay Prize. His published works include—*The Architecture of Humanism*; *A Box of Paints*; *Portrait of Zélide*, and *Poems*.

SITWELL, EDITH (1887). Born at Scarborough. Educated privately. Edited with her brothers an Anthology of Modern Verse called *Wheels*, which was marked by violent revolt against the popular poetry of the time. Her published works include—*The Mother and Other Poems*; *Clowns' Houses*; *The Wooden Pegasus*; *Bucolic Comedies*; *The Sleeping Beauty*; *Troy Park*; *Rustic Elegies*; *Alexander Pope*; *Collected Poems*; *The Pleasures of Poetry*; *Bath*; *The English Eccentrics*; *Victoria of England*, and *Aspects of Modern Poetry*.

SITWELL, OSBERT (1892). Born in London. Educated at Eton. Grenadier Guards, 1913–1919. His published works include—*The Winstonburg Line*; *Three Satires*; *Argonaut and Juggernaut*; *Out of the Flame*; *Before the Bombardment* (a novel); *England Reclaimed*; *Collected Poems and Satires*; *Miracle on Sinai* (a novel); and *Winters of Content*. Has contributed to various periodicals.

SPENDER, STEPHEN (1909). Educated at University College School, Hampstead, and University College, Oxford. Has travelled widely in Europe—two years in Germany, after Oxford. His published works include—*Poems*; *The Destructive Element*; *Vienna*; *The Burning Cactus*; *Forward from Liberalism*, and *Death of a Judge*.

STRONG, LEONARD ALFRED GEORGE (1896). Born at Plympton. Educated at Brighton College, and Wadham College, Oxford. Assistant master at Summerfields Preparatory School, Oxford. His published works include—*Dublin Days*; *The Lowery Road*; *Difficult Love*, *Northern Light* (poems); *Dewer Rides*; *The English Captain*; *The Garden*; *The Brothers*; *Sea Wall*; *Corporal Tune* (fiction), and *Life in English Literature* (criticism).

STRUTHER, JAN (Mrs. Joyce Maxtone-Graham) (1901). Educated privately. Has been contributing since 1917 poems, articles, and short stories to various periodicals, including *Punch*, *The Spectator*, *The New Statesman*, and *The London Mercury*. Her published works include—*Betsinda Dances and Other Poems*; *Sycamore Square and Other Verses*, *The Modern Struwwelpeter* and *Mrs. Miniver*.

BIOGRAPHICAL NOTES

STUART, DOROTHY MARGARET. Educated privately. Assumed her mother's maiden name of Stuart. F.R.S.L., D.M.S. of *Punch*. Won for Great Britain the Silver Medal of the International Literary Contests of the Eighth Olympiad, 1924, by her cycle of *Sword Songs*. Writes historical or literary essays and monographs, with occasional incursions into fiction. Her published works include—*Beasts Royal and Other Poems*; *Historical Songs and Ballads*; *The Boy through the Ages*; *Horace Walpole* (English Men of Letters); *Men and Women of the Middle Ages*; *England's Story*; *Christina Rossetti* (English Men of Letters); *Men and Women of Plantagenet England*; *The Girl through the Ages*; *The Map* (with E. V. Davenport); *Molly Lepell, Lady Harvey*, and *An Interlude in Porcelain* (with E. V. Davenport).

TESSIMOND, A. S. J. (1902). Born in Birkenhead. Educated at Birkenhead School, Charterhouse, and Liverpool University. Assistant Master, assistant bookseller, and copy-writer in London advertising agencies. His published works include—*The Walls of Glass*.

THOMAS, DYLAN (1914). Born in Swansea. Little or no official education or employment. Contributor of poems, stories, and reviews to English, Welsh, and American periodicals. His published works include—*18 Poems*; and *25 Poems*.

TURNER, WALTER JAMES (1889). Born in China. Educated at Scotch College, Melbourne, and privately in Munich, and Vienna. R.G.A. Musical critic of the *New Statesman*; dramatic critic of the *London Mercury*; and Literary Editor of the *Daily Herald*. His published works include—*The Hunter and Other Poems*; *The Man who Ate the Popomack* (a play); *The Landscape of Cytherea*; *The Seven Days of the Sun*; *Orpheus, or the Music of the Future*; *Beethoven*; *New Poems*; *The Pursuit of Psyche*; *Wagner*; *Jack and Jill*; *Berlioz*, and *Mozart*.

WALKER, JAMES (1911). Born in Ancoats, Manchester. Spent childhood and early 'teens on fairground, and at Festiniog County Intermediate School received "initiation" into poetry. Assistant Magistrates' Clerk at Blaenau Festiniog, North Wales. Has contributed to *Country Life*, and various periodicals.

WARNER, REX (1905). Educated at St. George's School, Harpenden, and Wadham College, Oxford. Teacher in England and Egypt. Has contributed poems and articles concerned with literary criticism, education, and politics to various left wing periodicals. His published works include—*Poems*, and *The Wild Goose Chase* (a novel).

BIOGRAPHICAL NOTES

WELLESLEY, DOROTHY VIOLET (Duchess of Wellington). Born at Croughton, Cheshire. Educated privately. Has contributed to numerous periodicals and anthologies. Her published works include—*Poems*; *Lost Lane*; *Genesis*; *Deserted House*; *Poems of Ten Years*; and *Life of Sir George Goldie* (a memoir). Editor of The Hogarth Living Poets Series, 1928–1932, and *The Annual*, 1929.

WHISTLER, LAURENCE (1912–1945). Educated at Stowe, and Balliol College, Oxford. Awarded the first of the King's Gold Medals for Poetry, 1934. His published works include —*Armed October and Other Poems*; *Four Walls*; *The Emperor Heart*, and *Vanbrugh, Architect and Dramatist* (a critical biography).

WOLFE, HUMBERT (1885–1940). C.B.E., C.B. Born in Milan. Educated at Bradford Grammar School, and Wadham College, Oxford. Principal Assistant Secretary, Ministry of Labour. His published works include—*London Sonnets*; *Kensington Gardens*; *Humoresque*; *Requiem*; *This Blind Rose*; *Dialogues and Monologues*; *Snow*; *Now a Stranger* (autobiography); *Reverie of a Policeman*; *Sonnets for Helen* (translated from Ronsard); *Portraits by Inference* (experiments in biography); *Cyrano de Bergerac*.

YEATS, WILLIAM BUTLER (1865–1939). Born in Dublin. Educated at Godolphin School, Hammersmith, and Erasmus Smith School, Dublin. Studied Art in Dublin. Helped to establish the Irish National Theatre in 1899, for which he wrote *Plays for an Irish Theatre*. Awarded the Nobel Prize for Literature, 1923. His published works include—*The Wanderings of Oisin*; *The Countess Cathleen*; *The Celtic Twilight* (essays); *Poems*; *Prose* (Collected Edition); *Later Poems*; *The Tower*; *The Winding Stair*; *Collected Poems*; *Collected Plays*; *Wheels and Butterflies*, and *A Full Moon in March*.

YOUNG, ANDREW (1885), Born in Elgin. Educated at the Royal High School, and the University of Edinburgh. His published works include—*The Cuckoo Clock*; *Thirty-one Poems*; *The Adversary* (a dramatic poem); *The Birdcage*; *The New Shepherd*; *Winter Harvest*, and *White Blackbird*.

POEMS OF TO-DAY

THIRD SERIES

LASCELLES ABERCROMBIE

1. *The Stream's Song*

MAKE way, make way,
You thwarting stones;
Room for my play,
Serious ones.

Do you not fear,
O rocks and boulders,
To feel my laughter
On your grave shoulders?

Do you not know
My joy at length
Will all wear out
Your solemn strength?

You will not for ever
Cumber my play;
With joy and a song
I clear my way.

Your faith of rock
Shall yield to me,
And be carried away
By the song of my glee.

LASCELLES ABERCROMBIE

Crumble, crumble,
Voiceless things ;
No faith can last
That never sings.

For the last hour
To joy belongs ;
The steadfast perish,
But not the songs.

Yet for a while
Thwart me, O boulders ;
I need for laughter
Your serious shoulders.

And when my singing
Has razed you quite,
I shall have lost
Half my delight.

J. REDWOOD ANDERSON

2. *The Bell*

STEADILY, steadily,
across the rapid estuary
the keen East wind blew from the sea :
breath of the unapparent sun
from regions of the New-Begun
to the old lands of Dead-and-Done.

The church-clock in its ancient tower,
cracked and wheezing, told the hour ;

then the bell began to ring
for early weekday worshipping.

The ploughman, muffled half in dream,
plodding slow behind his team,
the cowman, shuffling to his stall,
heard, but heeded not, the call ;
only three old women heard
—beat of bell and pipe of bird—
three grey Marys crooked and bent
who took their way at break of day
to taste their dead Lord's sacrament.

I, too, heard it, where I listened
by the hedge along the road,
where the spangled cobweb glistened
on the grasses at my feet,
and the dew-pearl palely glowed
like an infant newly christened ;
heard the sharp insistent beat :
Taste the Lord, and see how sweet !

Listening, heard, until the last
throb of summons, fainting, passed
—to a ghost of ringing thinned—
down the deserts of the wind ;
silence fell, save for the rush
of windy voices saying Hush,
and one last thin pipe of bird,
and in that silence I heard well
the beating of another bell :
upon the wind, a changing note,
faint, tumultuous, sharp, remote.

J. REDWOOD ANDERSON

A sound of danger ringing free
across the rapid estuary,
a sudden hope, a sudden doubt;
a sound of challenge ringing wide
to the drowsy country-side:
the bell-buoy, as it swayed about
on the river's breast, far out
where the river meets the sea.

Faint, remote and turbulent,
Summons to what Sacrament?
Invitation to assist
at what wilder Eucharist,
what primeval Table spread
with elemental Wine and Bread?
Sanctus when what Bread and Wine
flash to Substances divine?
Cup of Time and Host of Space,
Hope of Glory, Means of Grace—
what new God here showed his face?

What strange Bridal? Kiss sublime?
what Assumption of the Soul?
what Drowning in the Seas that roll
from coast to utter coast of time?

What Adventure of the Spirit,
new Goal set and new Crown given?
what new earth, new sea, new heaven,
for Life's Foundling to inherit?
Horizons where the sea and sky
meet and merge in ecstasy;

horizons where the great tides run
blood-tinctured by the risen sun ;
horizons where the soul is caught
beyond all sense, beyond all thought,
made one with the First Force of things
past even love's imaginings.

The ploughman, muffled yet in dream,
plodding slow behind his team,
the cowman, shuffling out of stall,
heeded not, nor heard, the call.

Steadily, steadily,
across the rapid estuary
the keen East wind blows from the sea.

W. H. AUDEN

3. *Fish in the Unruffled Lakes*

FISH in the unruffled lakes
The swarming colours wear,
Swans in the winter air
A white perfection have,
And the great lion walks
Through his innocent grove ;
Lion, fish, and swan
Act, and are gone
Upon Time's toppling wave.

We till shadowed days are done,
We must weep and sing

Duty's conscious wrong,
The Devil in the clock,
The Goodness carefully worn
For atonement or for luck ;
We must lose our loves,
On each beast and bird that moves
Turn an envious look.

Sighs for folly said and done
Twist our narrow days ;
But I must bless, I must praise
That you, my swan, who have
All gifts that to the swan
Impulsive Nature gave,
The majesty and pride,
Last night should add
Your voluntary love.

4. *Look, Stranger*

LOOK, stranger, at this island now
The leaping light for your delight discovers,
Stand stable here
And silent be,
That through the channels of the ear
May wander like a river
The swaying sound of the sea.

Here at the small field's ending pause
Where the chalk wall falls to the foam, and its tall ledges
Oppose the pluck
And knock of the tide,

And the shingle scrambles after the suck-
ing surf, and the gull lodges
A moment on its sheer side.

Far off like floating seeds the ships
Diverge on urgent voluntary errands ;
And the full view
Indeed may enter
And move in memory as now these clouds do,
That pass the harbour mirror
And all the summer through the water saunter.

5. *O what is that Sound*

O WHAT is that sound which so thrills the ear
Down in the valley drumming, drumming ?
Only the scarlet soldiers, dear,
The soldiers coming.

O what is that light I see flashing so clear
Over the distance brightly, brightly ?
Only the sun on their weapons, dear,
As they step lightly.

O what are they doing with all that gear ;
What are they doing this morning, this morning ?
Only the usual manœuvres, dear,
Or perhaps a warning.

O why have they left the road down there ;
Why are they suddenly wheeling, wheeling ?
Perhaps a change in the orders, dear ;
Why are you kneeling ?

O haven't they stopped for the doctor's care;
  Haven't they reined their horses, their horses?
Why, they are none of them wounded, dear,
    None of these forces.

O is it the parson they want with white hair;
  Is it the parson, is it, is it?
No, they are passing his gateway, dear,
    Without a visit.

O it must be the farmer who lives so near;
  It must be the farmer so cunning, so cunning?
They have passed the farm already, dear,
    And now they are running.

O where are you going? stay with me here!
  Were the vows you swore me deceiving, deceiving?
No, I promised to love you, dear,
    But I must be leaving.

O it's broken the lock and splintered the door,
  O it's the gate where they're turning, turning;
Their feet are heavy on the floor
    And their eyes are burning.

6. *Lay your Sleeping Head*

LAY your sleeping head, my love,
Human on my faithless arm;
Time and fevers burn away
Individual beauty from
Thoughtful children, and the grave

Proves the child ephemeral:
But in my arms till break of day
Let the living creature lie,
Mortal, guilty, but to me
The entirely beautiful.

Soul and body have no bounds:
To lovers as they lie upon
Her tolerant enchanted slope
In their ordinary swoon,
Grave the vision Venus sends
Of supernatural sympathy,
Universal love and hope;
While an abstract insight wakes
Among the glaciers and the rocks
The hermit's sensual ecstasy.

Certainty, fidelity
On the stroke of midnight pass
Like vibrations of a bell,
And fashionable madmen raise
Their pedantic boring cry;
Every farthing of the cost,
All the dreaded cards foretell
Shall be paid, but from this night
Not a whisper, not a thought,
Not a kiss nor look be lost.

Beauty, midnight, vision dies:
Let the winds of dawn that blow
Softly round your dreaming head
Such a day of sweetness show
Eye and knocking heart may bless,

Find the mortal world enough;
Noons of dryness see you fed
By the involuntary powers,
Nights of insult let you pass
Watched by every human love.

7. *Song for the New Year*

IT'S farewell to the drawing-room's civilised cry
The professor's sensible whereto and why
The frock-coated diplomat's social aplomb
Now matters are settled with gas and with bomb.

The works for two pianos, the brilliant stories
Of reasonable giants and remarkable fairies,
The pictures, the ointments, the frangible wares,
And the branches of olive are stored upstairs.

For the Devil has broken parole and arisen,
He has dynamited his way out of prison,
Out of the well where his Papa throws
The rebel angel, the outcast rose.

Like influenza he walks abroad,
He stands on the bridge, he waits by the ford;
As a goose or a gull he flies overhead,
He hides in the cupboards and under the bed.

Assuming such shapes as may best disguise
The hate that burns in his big blue eyes;
He may be a baby that croons in its pram,
Or a dear old grannie boarding a tram:

W. H. AUDEN

A plumber, a doctor, for he has his skill
To adopt a serious profession at will;
Superb at ice-hockey, a prince at the dance,
He's fierce as the tiger, secretive as plants.

O were he to triumph, dear heart, you know
To what depths of shame he would drag you low;
He would steal you away from me, yes, my dear,
He would steal you and cut off your marvellous hair.

Millions already have come to their harm,
Succumbing like doves to his adder's charm:
Hundreds of trees in the wood are unsound;
I'm the axe that must cut them down to the ground.

For I, after all, am the fortunate one,
The Happy-go-Lucky, the spoilt third son;
For me it is written the Devil to chase,
And to rid the earth of the human race.

The behaving of man is a world of horror,
A sedentary Sodom and slick Gomorrah:
I must take charge of the liquid fire
And storm the cities of human desire;

The buying and selling, the eating and drinking,
The disloyal machines and irreverent thinking,
The lovely dullards again and again
Inspiring their bitter ambitious men.

I shall come, I shall punish, the Devil be dead:
I shall have caviare thick on my bread,
I shall build myself a cathedral for home
With a vacuum cleaner in every room.

I shall ride on the front in a platinum car,
My features shall shine, my name shall be Star:
Day long and night long the bells I shall peal,
And down the long street I shall turn the cart-wheel.

So Little John, Long John, Polly and Peg,
And poor little Horace with only one leg,
You must leave your breakfast, your desk, and your
  play
On a fine summer morning the Devil to slay.

For it's order and trumpet and anger and drum,
And power and glory command you to come:
The graves shall fly open and suck you all in
And the earth shall be emptied of mortal sin.

The fishes are silent deep in the sea,
The skies are lit up like a Christmas tree,
The star in the West shoots its warning cry:
" Mankind is alive, but mankind must die."

So good-bye to the house with its wallpaper red,
Good-bye to the sheets on the warm double bed,
Good-bye to the beautiful birds on the wall,
It's good-bye, dear heart, good-bye to you all.

8. *There are some Birds in these Valleys*

THERE are some birds in these valleys
  Who flutter round the careless
With intimate appeal,
By seeming kindness trained to snaring,
They feel no falseness.

Under the spell completely
They circle can serenely,
And in the tricky light
The masked hill has a purer greenness.
Their flight looks fleeter.

But fowlers, O, like foxes,
Lie ambushed in the rushes.
Along the harmless tracks
The madman keeper crawls through brushwood,
Axe under oxter.

Alas, the signal given,
Fingers on trigger tighten.
The real unlucky dove
Must smarting fall away from brightness
Its love from living.

9. *Blues*

STOP all the clocks, cut off the telephone ;
Prevent the dog from barking with a juicy bone ;
Silence the pianos, and with muffled drum
Bring out the coffin, let the mourners come.

Let aeroplanes circle a moaning overhead,
Scribbling on the sky the message : " He is dead."
Put crêpe bows round the white necks of the public
doves ;
Let the traffic policemen wear black cotton gloves.

He was my North, my South, and East and West,
My working week, and my Sunday rest ;

My noon, my midnight, my talk, my song ;
I thought that love could last for ever : I was wrong.

The stars are not wanted now, put out every one ;
Pack up the moon and dismantle the sun ;
Pour away the ocean, and sweep up the wood :
For nothing now can ever come to any good.

GEORGE BARKER

10. *Bamborough Castle*

HERE where no house no home is I stand,
Looking down the sea lines of the island ;
The mountains against the shore where the lions' locks
Engarland in gold coils the great rocks,
And the flower precariously over the cliff edge leans.
I stand taking the air of the fountaining sea
That sends up its salt and foam over me,
While westward where no winds pester, the gulls
Fall slowly downward, and rest on the waves' hands.

Yes and behind me I hear the sore-throated crows
Creating their ruins of sound in the air by the ruins ;
By Bamborough's ruins they rise and brood, or
Poising in the air roar down at Promethean stone.
I see them deliver an excrement of blood as they pass
Or pitch their cries to crack the rock like glass :
But the stone holds and the blood's white, and I, alone,
Turning to discern the Bamborough mass,
See wall and window and all solid as stone,
Nor mess of blood smearing the gutted face.

Then I know what it is I look upon like a ruin,
The dilapidated palace on the promontory.
I know what each stone is, and the Portland walls,
The well like flute and diseased dungeon cells.
What is it but me, but you, but you all,—
Any man's many of days that make my life.
His day stones and year walls and his tower,
His flute of love and the festering cells of evil,
All worn dangerous to trespassers, and the ghosts
The consumptive and prophetic crows infest,
Investing his pile of life with mess, their cries
Threatening to raze him like the glass's bubble.

There where no house no home is I stood,
Bamborough I, cracked open and crowned with blood,
Disfigured by the birds I knew were no birds,
But the heart haunting crow who kills with words.

11. *Paradisiacal Bird*

PARADISIACAL bird
Of plumage flame
Poised upon the bough
Of glimmering bone

Whose wings of love
Spread on the azur
Of Time, traverse
All space with ease :

Flame with all glory
Life-phoenix, against

The awful and dark falling
Time of Death.

12. *The Seal Boy*

SEE he slips like insinuations
Into the waves and sidles
Across breakers, diving under
The greater tidals,

Plunging, a small plane
Down dark altitudes,
Trailing bubbles like aerial bombs
Or a balloon's broods.

O moving ecstatic boy
Sliding through the gloomy seas
Who bring me pearls to enjoy
Rarer than to be found in these seas—

Between the fixed bars of your lips
Darts the kiss like silver
Fish, and in my wild grip
You harbour, for ever.

13. *The Leaping Laughers*

WHEN will men again
Lift irresistible fists
Not bend from ends
But each man lift men
Nearer again.

GEORGE BARKER

Many men mean
Well : but tall walls
Impede, their hands bleed and
They fall, their seed the
Seed of the fallen.

See here the fallen
Stooping over stones, over their
Own bones : but all
Stooping doom beaten.

Whom the noonday washes
Whole, whom the heavens compel,
And to whom pass immaculate messages,
When will men again
Lift irresistible fists
Impede impediments
Leap mountains laugh at walls ?

JULIAN BELL

14. *Nonsense*

SING a song of sixpence,
A pocketful of rye,
The lover's in the garden
And battle's in the sky.
The banker's in the city
Getting off his gold ;
Oh isn't it a pity
The rye can't be sold.

JULIAN BELL

The queen is drinking sherry
And dancing to a band ;
A crowd may well feel merry
That it does not understand.

The banker turns his gold about
But that won't sell the rye,
Starve and grow cold without,
And ask the reason why
The guns are in the garden,
And battle's in the sky.

LAURENCE BINYON

15. *Mediterranean Verses*

I

THE desert sands at day's swift flight
Drank of the dew-cold vivid night
Where Nile flows as he flowed
When first men reaped and sowed,

As though his stream since Time began
Bore all the history of Man,
Vast ages lapsing brief
As noiseless as a leaf.

But when the first high star, concealed
By shadowing leaves above, revealed
The glinting ripple, it seemed
As the great water streamed

That ears attuned might hear the strings
Plucked by the harpist for those kings
Who in persistence fond
Would be companion'd

Through the faint under-world, and still
Press the firm-clustered grape and feel
Wind from the fanning plume
Sweetened with incense-fume ;

Still watch the honey-coloured grain
Stiffen to ripeness on the plain
Or dancers with slim flanks
Circle in chiming ranks.

For Time, so old, must abdicate.
Eyes and a smile that have no date
Respond from chiselled stone
Young as, each day, the dawn ;

And pullings of the carver's wrist
So subtly in those curves persist,
The presence in the form
To touch is almost warm.

But like the pictures dreams make glow
On darkness, that in daylight go
So soon except they find
Some lodging in the mind,

Only by beauty can these cross
The dark stream of the dead to us.
Only the hot sun dwells
'Mid those long parallels

Of broken pillars, roofed with air,
In temples of unanswered prayer ;
And Gods unfeasted own
Naught but a granite throne.

II

Rain and the scolding wind's uproar
And the black cloud befitted more
The towering walls that hem
Teeming Jerusalem ;

City of wailing, wrath, and blood,
The city of the grave and shroud
Whence arose the Word
That brought so sharp a sword.

O city stubbornly enthroned !
The city that the prophets stoned,
Over which Jesus wept
And proud Rome vainly swept.

But peace unearthly beamed above
As from a brooding heaven of love
The hill-surrounded sea
Of lonely Galilee.

And we beneath those silent skies
Walked among flowers of Paradise
As if their happier seed
Knew peace on earth indeed.

Peace, by the world praised and eschewed,
Lived in that ageless solitude

And with no phrases deckt
Shone richer in neglect ;

And under stony hills severe,
Where sounds are few, we still could hear
The shepherd from the rock
Pipe to his wandering flock.

Remote beyond the Syrian bay
At close of a long burning day
Into the dusk still shone
The snows of Lebanon.

III

Morning came dancing, Morning warmed
The blue sea-circle, whence she charmed
Isle after isle to rise
Rock-pointed toward the skies,

Whose names transfigured strand and cape
Into a legendary shape
Re-peopled from afar
But to be brought more near ;

As if old ships and oar'd galleys
Still swept along the silent seas ;
Sailors of Tyre in quest
Of the remoter West ;

The quick Athenian ; those who made
Adventure of the long crusade,
And Cleopatra's sail
From Actium flying pale ;

And traffickers with old Byzance
Past Patmos fading lost in trance ;
And Paul afire within
The sad world's soul to win ;

And doomed Othello Cyprus-bound.
The islands rose and sank around,
And when the day declined
Their shadows filled the mind.

Dim in the dawn stood Hector's ghost
Upon the mound where Troy lies lost.
But through the straits we sped
Turned to our dearer dead.

IV

The hills divide, the seas unite
The valleys of a land of light,
But O how bare beside
That Hellas glorified

Which, wasted, clan by warring clan,
Yet made a splendour shine in Man
By that inquiring will
Whose way we follow still ;

Built in the mind his palace rare,
Towered high as thought can dare
And thronged with images
Of joys and agonies,

Confronting destiny and wrong
With the high-symbol'd scene, and song

Threading its music through
The dark tale, else untrue.

But Time, so tender to a thought
That branches up from living root,
Has here unbuilt, defaced,
And Beauty dispossessed,

Conniving with men's minds inert,
Brute blows, and stupid skill to hurt,
As if 'twere half their joy
To maim and to destroy.

O Delphi, where all Hellas came
To hear the awful Voice proclaim
Fate, how beneath your steep
Is all-forgetting sleep !

No voice, no votary, no shrine ;
Though the long vale be still divine
From that blue bay below
To the far mountain snow,

And soundless noon that idly warms
The scattered stones and shattered forms
Only the shadow brings
Of wheeling eagles' wings.

V

In the last light a column glows
Where once the white perfection rose
Imperfectly divined
By the rebuilding mind

Which treasures up a shape, a thought,
From footprint or from echo caught,
Hard gleanings that attest
Oblivion has the best.

Fade coasts and isles, where the seed sown
Still flowers in all we are and own.
A future presses near
Clouds of unshapen fear.

And now the ghostly, vast night-fall
Like an age closing past recall
Seems, and this darkening sea
The wastes of history ;

The sea that no proud trophy claims
For sunken ventures, foundered fames,
Dishevelled navies tost,
Ships like a bubble lost ;

That keeps no sure abiding form
And rises in unconscious storm
Whipt by an ignorant blast
And when the fury's past

Sleeking its waves, mile after mile,
Into the image of a smile.
Is this what Time does still,
Working a witless will ?

But through the dark, stopt by no seas,
Pass other Powers and Presences
Unseen from shore to shore,
Armed and at conscious war,

Ideas, mightier than men,
That seize and madden, free or chain.
The things unprophesied
Are certain, naught beside.

But end is none, though the storms break
And the mind pale, and the heart shake.
Out of that future ring
Far trumpets challenging.

EDMUND BLUNDEN

16. *Bells*

WHAT master singer, with what glory amazed,
Heard one day listening on the lonely air
The tune of bells ere yet a bell was raised
To throne it over field and flood ? Who dare
Deny him demi-god, that so could win
The music uncreate, that so could wed
Music and hue—till, when the bells begin,
Song colours, colour sings ? Beauty so bred
Enspheres each hamlet through the English shires,
And utters from ten thousand peeping spires
(Or huge in starlight) to the outmost farms
Sweet, young, grand, old. The country's lustiest
arms
Leap to the time till the whole sky retells
That unknown poet's masterpiece of bells.

17. *April Byeway*

FRIEND whom I never saw, yet dearest friend,
  Be with me travelling on the byeway now
In April's month and mood : our steps shall bend
  By the shut smithy with its penthouse brow
  Armed round with many a felly and crackt plough :
And we will mark in his white smock the mill
  Standing aloof, long numbed to any wind,
That in his crannies mourns, and craves him still ;
  But now no fortune sends him grain to grind,
  And even the master lies too deep for winds to find.

Grieve not at these : for there are mills amain
  With lusty sails that leap and drop away
On further knolls, strong backs to fetch the grain.
  The schoolboys' wickets on the green betray
  New games begun and old ones put away.
Let us fare on, dead friend, O deathless friend,
  Where under his old hat as green as moss
The hedger chops and finds new gaps to mend,
  And on his bonfires burns the thorns and dross,
  And hums a hymn, the best, thinks he, that ever was.

There the grey guinea-fowl stands in the way,
  The young black heifer and the raw-ribbed mare,
Scorning to move for tumbril or for dray—
  They feel themselves as good as farmers there.
  From the young corn the prick-eared leverets stare
At strangers come to spy the land—small sirs,
  We bring less danger than the very breeze

Who in great zig-zag blows the bee, and whirs
  In bluebell shadow down the bright green leas ;
  From whom in frolic fit the chopt straw darts and flees.

The cherry steepling up in white shall know
  The two friends passing by, and poplar smile
All gold within ; the church-top fowl shall glow
  To lure us on, and we shall rest awhile
  Where the wild apple blooms above the stile ;
The yellow frog beneath blinks up half bold,
  Then scares himself into the deeper green.
And thus spring was for you in days of old,
  And thus will be should I too walk unseen
  By one that thinks me friend, the best that there has
      been.

All our lone journey laughs for joy, the hours
  Like honey-bees go home in new-found light
Past the cow-pond amazed with twinkling flowers
  And antique chalk-pit newly delved to white,
  Or idle snow-plough nearly hid from sight.
The blackbird sings us home, on a sudden peers
  The round tower hung with ivy's blackened chains,
Then past the little green the byeway veers,
  The mill-sweeps torn, the forge with cobwebbed
      panes
  That have so many years looked out across the plains.

But the old forge and mill are shut and done,
  The tower is crumbling down, stone by stone falls ;
An ague doubt comes creeping in the sun,
  The sun becomes a ghost, the day appals,
  The concourse of a thousand tempests sprawls

Over the blue-lipped lakes and maddening groves,
  Like agonies of gods the clouds are whirled,
The stormwind like the demon huntsman roves—
  Still stands my friend, though all's to chaos hurled,
  The unseen friend, the one last friend in all the world.

18. *Values*

TILL darkness lays a hand on these gray eyes
  And out of man my ghost is sent alone,
It is my chance to know that force and size
Are nothing but by answered undertone.
No beauty even of absolute perfection
Dominates here—the glance, the pause, the guess
Must be my amulets of resurrection;
Raindrops may murder, lightnings may caress.

There I was tortured, but I cannot grieve;
There crowned and palaced—visibles deceive.
That storm of belfried cities in my mind
Leaves me my vespers cool and eglantined.
From love's wide-flowering mountain-side I chose
This sprig of green, in which an angel shows.

CICELY BOAS

19. *The Gentleman in Yellow*

THE lady on the mantelpiece had flowers in her lap;
  She wore a dainty yellow gown and ribbons in her
    cap;

CICELY BOAS

I was always rather sorry that the mantel was so wide,
Because the yellow gentleman lived right the other side.
He was such a pretty fellow,
And he had a little 'cello,
And he would have liked the yellow
Little lady for his bride.

They lived there all alone, with just a pair of Toby jugs,
And a graded row—like organ pipes—of big and little mugs
Which I filled with yellow daffodils and kingcups in the spring,
And sometimes when I'd gone away the gentleman would sing.
He was such a merry fellow,
Till I went and bought Othello
And the Meissen Punchinello,
And they ruined everything.

When the summer sun was shining and the buttercups in bloom
I used to fill the Toby jugs with spikes of yellow broom,
And the gentleman would fiddle till the day when things went wrong
And the little yellow lady wouldn't listen to his song.
Was she smiling at Othello
Or the Meissen Punchinello
That the gentleman in yellow
Had to play in vain so long?

And when autumn filled the garden I arranged the plumy sheaves
Of asphodel and golden rod and yellow autumn leaves

CICELY BOAS

In the mugs upon the mantel, where they mingled in a
 hedge
Behind the little figures standing silent on the ledge;
  And I wondered if Othello
  Or the Meissen Punchinello
  Pushed the gentleman in yellow
  So very near the edge?

It may be she was fickle, so perhaps it served her right,
But this morning, when I filled the mugs with winter
 aconite,
I found the yellow lady, who had seemed so coy of late,
Bewailing very bitterly her little partner's fate.
  For she didn't love Othello
  Or the Meissen Punchinello—
  And the gentleman in yellow
  Is in pieces in the grate.

GUY BOAS

20. *To a Bicycle Bell*

ALAS, how many years have flown
 Since first your silvery note I sounded,
And on a cycle of my own
 First o'er the bumps in boyhood bounded,
And felt, like Icarus, the delight
Of suddenly acquiring flight.

The roads were peaceful then; no noise
 More strident than your ring intruded,

And bells of other little boys
  Who also cycled (as a few did),
And those of elder people who
Sedately pedalled two-and-two.

But the inventive brain of man,
  As restless as the winds that fan it,
Is always making some new plan
  To work commotion on our planet;
Especially it thinks we need
Devices for increasing speed.

So motors came, and all was turned
  From peace to uproar in a twinkle;
The tempest blew, the waves were churned;
  Your modest and melodious tinkle,
Where hooters hoot and klaxons squall,
Can scarcely now be heard at all.

Lorries and motor-buses dash
  Along the road which was my cycle's,
And charabancs about me crash,
  Sounding a trump as loud as Michael's;
Amid the din it is absurd
To try to make your tinkle heard.

When in the future I retire
  (So runs my fanciful reflection)
And find some land of heart's desire
  Where everything will be perfection,
Motors shall vanish like a dream
And cycles be once more supreme.

Then once again, my bell, you'll serve
  To warn pedestrians encroaching
Upon my path. You'll not unnerve,
  But sweetly hint that I'm approaching,
Nor, like the horn, instil dismay
Into the people in the way.

Gently I'll pedal through the town
  And down the flowering lanes and by-ways,
And nobody shall fly or frown
  At meeting me upon the highways,
And even sergeants of police
Shall smile upon my wheels of peace.

And children, looking close, will tell
  From signs beneath my looks seraphic
That, Dante-like, I've been in hell—
  The hell of England's post-war traffic;
And they will make it extra nice
For one returned to Paradise.

21. *Doubt*

DESCARTES laid it down that a person may doubt
  The existence of everything under the sun
Except of oneself: there's no doubting about
  The contrivance through which all the doubting is
    done.
This subtle, suggestive but puzzling remark
  In so many directions the lecturer twisted
That he ended by leaving us all in the dark,
  For he caused us to doubt whether DESCARTES
    existed.

22. *Ploughing*

EARLY and pregnant hour;
Hazily sunbeams lacquer
The flanks of horses ploughing the Fourteen Acre.
They move in a cocoon of golden steam,
The logical furrow following furled and spare.
I saw the countryman tough behind his team,
And paused to stare
At his long shadow in Time, his tangent power.

23. *The Hedge-row Story*

WHEN fields here lose their colour, when the wood
trailing a hoary wing turns home
to raven night, I reckon up the sum
of rustic evil and clay-spattered good.

I think of the innumerable slow lives whose history
differs a hairsbreadth from the hedge-row story:
thorns in black competition, the roped glory
of gossamer, soon gone,
with berries dipped in blood.

When fields here lose the light, I fear the mystery
of men like trees, that tower but touch the sky
they cannot and are felled one by one,
I think of saint and scarecrow schooled to die;
their leafless victory stands, where nothing stood.

A. C. BOYD

24. *Maritime Invocation*

LADY, will you go with me
over the dark, the wave-demented sea?
Lady, I must tell you
how frail love's boat is,
I must bring to your notice
the skulls on the beach,
the spars, foam-flecked, of ships wrecked.

Lady, are you brave enough
to go on such a journey?
You will be safe enough,
your hand in mine, till you know
that passion's star is a falling star,
and passion's voice a lost voice calling far
into the dark and getting no reply.

Ah! lady, though touch may fail us,
waves intervening,
there is no night so outrageous
that our minds battened together
may not weather,
our hearts morticed as one rudder,
keel set towards love's horizon.
Lady, the dawn, the dawn shall break there,
and the sun shall rise on these dangerous,
these tide-torn waters.

Lady, will you go out with me
on such a journey, and in such a sea?

ROBERT BRIDGES

25. *Cheddar Pinks*

MID the squander'd colour
  idling as I lay
Reading the Odyssey
  in my rock-garden
I espied the cluster'd
  tufts of Cheddar pinks
Burgeoning with promise
  of their scented bloom
All the modish motley
  of their bloom to be
Thrust up in narrow buds
  on the slender stalks.
Thronging springing urgent
  hasting (so I thought)
As if they feared to be
  too late for summer—
Like schoolgirls overslept
  waken'd by the bell
Leaping from bed to don
  their muslin dresses
    On a May morning:

Then felt I like to one
  indulging in sin
(Whereto Nature is oft
  a blind accomplice)
Because my aged bones
  so enjoyed the sun

ROBERT BRIDGES

There as I lay along
  idling with my thoughts
Reading an old poet
  while the busy world
Toil'd moil'd fuss'd and scurried
  worried bought and sold
Plotted stole and quarrel'd
  fought and God knows what.
I had forgotten Homer
  dallying with my thoughts
Till I fell to making
  these little verses
Communing with the flowers
  in my rock-garden
    On a May morning.

HILTON BROWN

26. *To a Panther*

"BEHOLD, the felon Pard hath slain a goat
  Whereof he hath but tasted ; which thereby
  He must revisit." So they spoke, and I,
Hopeful, allowed alluring dreams to float
  Before mine eager eye—
A mounted head for me, a panther coat
For someone else, an honest evening's fun,
Hazard, an outlaw slain, a good deed truly done.

And so for love of you I left my camp
  And staggered weary miles into the blue
  And sat in a *machan* the long night through,

Eaten by ants and crucified by cramp.
And did you come ? Not you.
Phoebus went down and Dian raised her lamp ;
In solemn march the constellations passed ;
And now the dawn's afoot. . . . Home, John, ay, home
at last !

Confound you, Pard, you spotted insolent !
The feast was ready and the table spread ;
Why were you not by common cravings led,
By appetites and ravening hungers rent,
That clamoured to be fed ?
Why not have dined—or come with that intent
And trysted with the poor benighted bard,
Instead of backing out like this ? Oh, curse you, Pard !

And yet—and yet—so sweet, so passing fair,
So magical was this sequestered spot
(Of *your* selection) that the bard forgot,
So soon as evening wandered down the air,
He had been tired and hot ;
And sat bewitched and drank the nectar rare
Of dew and sunset and the scented flowers,
Till lastly rose the moon ; and then came fairy hours.

Came last the moon with solace in her train,
And thoughts that shun rude day's bedevillings,
And night-time fantasies on timid wings,
And but for you in slumber I had lain
Missing these lovely things ;
And, though you should, to crown it, have been slain,
I grudge you not your night of happiness,
For I—well, after all, I too have had no less.

HILTON BROWN

And so let's say all's happened for the best.
I'll to the homeward byways ghostly lit
With waning moonshine ; you the while may flit
Down scented glades on your eternal quest—
Lord give you joy of it !
And, though you would not come at my behest,
Let's hope you bag some fat upstanding buck.
Good hunting, friend, to you ; good night, dear Pard,
good luck !

ROY CAMPBELL

27. *Autumn*

I LOVE to see, when leaves depart,
The clear anatomy arrive,
Winter, the paragon of art,
That kills all forms of life and feeling
Save what is pure and will survive.

Already now the clanging chains
Of geese are harnessed to the moon :
Stripped are the great sun-clouding planes :
And the dark pines, their own revealing,
Let in the needles of the noon.

Strained by the gale the olives whiten
Like hoary wrestlers bent with toil
And, with the vines, their branches lighten
To brim our vats where summer lingers
In the red froth and sun-gold oil.

Soon on our hearth's reviving pyre
Their rotted stems will crumble up :
And like a ruby, panting fire,
The grape will redden on your fingers
Through the lit crystal of the cup.

28. *The Serf*

HIS naked skin clothed in the torrid mist
That puffs in smoke around the patient hooves,
The ploughman drives, a slow somnambulist,
And through the green his crimson furrow grooves.
His heart, more deeply than he wounds the plain,
Long by the rasping share of insult torn,
Red clod, to which the war-cry once was rain
And tribal spears the fatal sheaves of corn,
Lies fallow now. But as the turf divides
I see in the slow progress of his strides
Over the toppled clods and falling flowers,
The timeless, surly patience of the serf
That moves the nearest to the naked earth
And ploughs down palaces, and thrones, and towers.

29. *Horses on the Camargue*

IN the grey wastes of dread,
The haunt of shattered gulls where nothing moves
But in a shroud of silence like the dead,
I heard a sudden harmony of hooves,
And, turning, saw afar
A hundred snowy horses unconfined,

The silver runaways of Neptune's car
Racing, spray-curled, like waves before the wind.
Sons of the Mistral, fleet
As him with whose strong gusts they love to flee,
Who shod the flying thunders on their feet
And plumed them with the snortings of the sea ;
Theirs is no earthly breed
Who only haunt the verges of the earth
And only on the sea's salt herbage feed—
Surely the great white breakers gave them birth.
For when for years a slave,
A horse of the Camargue, in alien lands,
Should catch some far-off fragrance of the wave
Carried far inland from his native sands,
Many have told the tale
Of how in fury, foaming at the rein,
He hurls his rider ; and with lifted tail,
With coal-red eyes and cataracting mane,
Heading his course for home,
Though sixty foreign leagues before him sweep,
Will never rest until he breathes the foam
And hears the native thunder of the deep.
But when the great gusts rise
And lash their anger on these arid coasts,
When the scared gulls career with mournful cries
And whirl across the waste like driven ghosts :
When hail and fire converge,
The only souls to which they strike no pain
Are the white-crested fillies of the surge
And the white horses of the windy plain.
Then in their strength and pride
The stallions of the wilderness rejoice ;
They feel their Master's trident in their side,

And high and shrill they answer to his voice.
With white tails smoking free,
Long streaming manes, and arching necks, they show
Their kinship to their sisters of the sea—
And forward hurl their thunderbolts of snow.
Still out of hardship bred,
Spirits of power and beauty and delight
Have ever on such frugal pastures fed
And loved to course with tempests through the night.

G. M. COOKSON

30. *Peg-top Time*

PEG-TOP time has come again;
The air is rough and raw;
Green grows the wild plum down the lane,
Dull red the wrinkled haw.

Shrill to a sky of cinnamon
The cock of dawn has crowed;
And the wind is up like a poor man's son,
Free of the broad, bleak road.

The road that's white as a greybeard's face,
Long as a lawyer's bill;
And yet it is a lusty place
When the wind comes over the hill.

So jump, my joes in corduroys,
Or he will pinch you blue;

Romp with the wind, ye hardy boys,
And he will romp with you.

Dunce, here's a fellow to your pate ;
Crack on, you scholar quick ;
I guess the calculus of Fate
Beats your arithmetic.

But here the master of the ring
In childhood's magic O
With your top and your stick and your bit of string
Be happier than you know.

Old Time will plait you thicker thongs
And crunch with harder heel ;
This sunshine-hour to you belongs ;
You are the joy you feel.

31. *The Blind Sailor*

LEAD out the blind sailor that once was England's pride,
A bold man and a burly and a man of jest was he :
Lead out the blind sailor on the green hillside,
A pale light falling on the old gray sea.

Lead out the blind sailor ; go tenderly and slow,
For he is but a withered leaf was once a goodly tree ;
His feeble feet falter and his spirits are sunk low
That once were as a billow when the sun shines on the sea.

G. M. COOKSON

Lead on the blind sailor and let him feel the sun,
For weary will winter and the white fog be,
And the wind in the chimney sound like a warning
gun
When a blind ship crawls to her grave in the sea.

Lead home the blind sailor ; set him down by his fire-
side ;
And he'll pipe a cheerful song that's a sad song to me ;
And if I too grow dim-eyed my tears I need not hide,
For those salt drops of sorrow my sailor cannot see.

FRANCES CORNFORD

32. *A Glimpse*

O GRASSES wet with dew, yellow fallen leaves,
Smooth-shadowed waters Milton loved, green
banks,
Arched bridges, rooks, and rain-leaved willow-trees,
Stone, serious familiar colleges,
For ever mine.
The figure of a scholar carrying back
Books to the library—absorbed, content,
Seeming as everlasting as the elms
Bark-wrinkled, puddled round their roots, the bells,
And the far shouting in the football fields.

The same since I was born, the same to be
When all my children's children grow old men.

33. *The Mongrel*

YOUR Laurel Hedge, with its broad leaves,
  Keeps fresh and green from year to year;
While that poor Wayside, Mongrel hedge,
  In Winter time goes thin and bare.
But when October's in his prime,
  How beautiful that Mongrel grows—
Where Blackberry, Thorn and other leaves
  Can make a hundred shining hues!
In singles, twins, and triplets too,
  In bunch and cluster, high and low,
I see his fruits in heavy folds,
  Or fluttering lightly to and fro.
The Apple with her beauty-moles,
  The beady Currant, glassy-eyed;
The golden Corn, all naked there,
  Without a leaf on either side.
The nippled Pear and misty Plum,
  The yellow Quince and Cherry red;
The crimson Strawberry, full of dimples,
  Now lying so low in her bed.
Let no man touch this Mongrel now,
  Nor dare to pick his fruit, for fear
That Wizard turns his gorgeous feast
  To shrivelled leaves, all limp and sere.

34. *Frost*

WHAT swords and spears, what daggers bright
He arms the morning with! How light
His powder is, that's fit to lie
On the wings of a butterfly!
What milk-white clothing he has made
For every little twig and blade!
What curious silver work is shown
On wood and iron, glass and stone!
" If you, my slim Jack Frost, can trace
This work so fine, so full of grace,
Tell me," I said, " before I go—
Where is your plump young sister, Snow?"

35. *The Poet*

WHEN I went down past Charing Cross,
A plain and simple man was I;
I might have been no more than air,
Unseen by any mortal eye.

But, Lord in Heaven, had I the power
To show my inward spirit there,
Then what a pack of human hounds
Had hunted me, to strip me bare.

A human pack, ten thousand strong,
All in full cry to bring me down;
All greedy for my magic robe,
All crazy for my burning crown.

36. *The Ecstatic*

LARK, skylark, spilling your rubbed and round
Pebbles of sound in air's still lake,
Whose widening circles fill the noon ; yet none
Is known so small beside the sun :

Be strong your fervent soaring, your skyward air !
Tremble there, a nerve of song !
Float up there where voice and wing are one,
A singing star, a note of light !

Buoyed, embayed in heaven's noon-wide reaches—
For soon light's tide will turn—Oh stay !
Cease not till day streams to the west, then down
That estuary drop down to peace.

37. *Learning to Talk*

SEE this small one, tiptoe on
The green foothills of the years,
Views a younger world than yours ;
When you go down, he'll be the tall one.

Dawn's dew is on his tongue—
No word for what's behind the sky,
Naming all that meets the eye,
Pleased with sunlight over a lawn.

Hear his laughter. He can't contain
The exquisite moment overflowing.

Limbs leaping, woodpecker flying
Are for him and not hereafter.

Tongue trips, recovers, triumphs,
Turning all ways to express
What the forward eye can guess—
That time is his and earth young.

We are growing too like trees
To give the rising wind a voice :
Eagles shall build upon our verse,
Our winged seeds are to-morrow's sowing.

Yes, we learn to speak for all
Whose hearts here are not at home,
All who march to a better time
And breed the world for which they burn.

38. *A Time to Dance*

FOR those who had the power
   of the forest fires that burn
Leaving their source in ashes
   to flush the sky with fire :
Those whom a famous urn
   could not contain, whose passion
Brimmed over the deep grave
   and dazzled epitaphs :
For all that have won us wings
   to clear the tops of grief,
My friend who within me laughs
   bids you dance and sing.

Some set out to explore
  earth's limit, and little they recked if
Never their feet came near it
  outgrowing the need for glory :
Some aimed at a small objective
  but the fierce updraught of their spirit
Forced them to the stars.
  Are honoured in public who built
The dam that tamed a river ;
  or holding the salient for hours
Against odds, cut off and killed,
  are remembered by one survivor.

All these. But most for those
  whom accident made great,
As a radiant chance encounter
  of cloud and sunlight grows
Immortal on the heart :
  whose gift was the sudden bounty
Of a passing moment, enriches
  the fulfilled eye for ever.
Their spirits float serene
  above time's roughest reaches,
But their seed is in us and over
  our lives they are evergreen.

39. *When Nature plays Hedge-Schoolmaster*

WHEN nature plays hedge-schoolmaster,
  Shakes out the gaudy map of summer
And shows me charabanc, rose, barley-ear
And every bright-winged hummer,

CECIL DAY LEWIS

He only would require of me
To be the sponge of natural laws
And learn no more of that cosmography
Than passes through the pores.

Why must I then unleash my brain
To sweat after some revelation
Behind the rose, heedless if truth maintain
On the rose-bloom her station ?

When bullying April bruised mine eyes
With sleet-bound appetites and crude
Experiments of green, I still was wise
And kissed the blossoming rod.

Now summer brings what April took,
Riding with fanfares from the south,
And I should be no Solomon to look
My Sheba in the mouth.

Charabancs shout along the lane
And summer gales bay in the wood
No less superbly because I can't explain
What I have understood.

Let logic analyse the hive,
Wisdom's content to have the honey :
So I'll go bite the crust of things and thrive
While hedgerows still are sunny.

40. *Do not Expect again a Phœnix Hour*

DO not expect again a phœnix hour,
The triple-towered sky, the dove complaining,
Sudden the rain of gold and heart's first ease
Tranced under trees by the eldritch light of sundown.

By a blazed trail our joy will be returning :
One burning hour throws light a thousand ways,
And hot blood stays into familiar gestures.
The best years wait, the body's plenitude.

Consider then, my lover, this is the end
Of the lark's ascending, the hawk's unearthly hover :
Spring season is over soon and first heatwave ;
Grave-browed with cloud ponders the huge horizon.

Draw up the dew. Swell the pacific violence.
Take shape in silence. Grow as the clouds grew.
Beautiful brood the cornlands, and you are heavy ;
Leafy the boughs—they also hide big fruit.

41. *Oh Hush Thee, my Baby*

OH hush thee, my baby,
Thy cradle's in pawn :
No blankets to cover thee
Cold and forlorn.
The stars in the bright sky
Look down and are dumb
At the heir of the ages
Asleep in a slum.

CECIL DAY LEWIS

The hooters are blowing,
No heed let him take;
When baby is hungry
'Tis best not to wake.
Thy mother is crying,
Thy dad's on the dole:
Two shillings a week is
The price of a soul.

WALTER DE LA MARE

42. *A Robin*

GHOST-GREY the fall of night,
  Ice-bound the lane,
Lone in the dying light
  Flits he again;
Lurking where shadows steal,
Perched in his coat of blood,
Man's homestead at his heel,
  Death-still the wood.

Odd restless child; it's dark;
  All wings are flown
But this one wizard's—hark!—
  Stone clapped on stone!
Changeling and solitary,
Secret and sharp and small,
Flits he from tree to tree,
  Calling on all.

43. *The Little Creature*

TWINKUM, twankum, twirlum, twitch—
My great grandam—She was a Witch,
Mouse in Wainscot, Saint in niche—
My great grandam—She was a Witch;
Deadly nightshade flowers in a ditch—
My great grandam—She was a Witch;
Long though the shroud, it grows stitch by stitch—
My great grandam—She was a Witch;
Wean your weakling before you breech—
My great grandam—She was a Witch;
The fattest pig's but a double flitch—
My great grandam—She was a Witch;
Nightjars rattle, owls scritch—
My great grandam—She was a Witch.

Pretty and small,
A mere nothing at all,
Pinned up sharp in the ghost of a shawl,
She'd straddle her down to the kirkyard wall,
And mutter and whisper and call,
And call. . . .

Red blood out and black blood in,
My Nannie says I'm a child of sin.
How did I choose me my witchcraft kin?
Know I as soon as dark's dreams begin
Snared is my heart in a nightmare's gin;
Never from terror I out may win;
So—dawn and dusk—I pine, peak, thin,
Scarcely beknowing t'other from which—
My great grandam—She was a Witch.

44. *Snow*

THIS meal-white snow—
Oh, look at the bright fields,
What crystal manna
Death-cold winter yields!

Falling from heavens
Earth knows little of,
Yet mantling it
As with a flawless love–

A shining cloak—
It to the naked gives,
Wooing all sorrow
From the soul it shrives.

Adam no calmer vales
Than these descried,
Leda a shadow were
This white beside.

Water stays still for wonder;
Herb and flower,
Else starved with cold,
In warmth and darkness cower.

Miracle, far and near,
That starry flake
Can of its myriads
Such wide pastures make,

For sun to colour
And for moon to wan,

And day's vast vault of blue
To arch upon!

A marvel of light,
Whose verge of radiance seems
Frontier of paradise,
The bourne of dreams.

O tranquil, silent, cold—
Such loveliness to see:
The heart sighs answer,
Benedicite!

JOHN DRINKWATER

45. *Who were before Me*

LONG time in some forgotten churchyard earth of Warwickshire,
My fathers in their generations lie beyond desire,
And nothing breaks the rest, I know, of John Drinkwater now,
Who left in sixteen-seventy his roan team at plough.

And James, son of John, is there, a mighty ploughman too,
Skilled he was at thatching and the barleycorn brew,
And he had a heart-load of sorrow in his day,
But ten score of years ago he put it away.

Then Thomas came, and played a fiddle cut of mellow wood,

And broke his heart, they say, for love that never
came to good.
A hundred winter peals and more have rung above
his bed—
O, poor eternal grief, so long, so lightly, comforted.

And in the gentle yesterday these were but glimmering
tombs,
Or tales to tell on fireside eves of legendary dooms;
I being life while they were none, what had their dust
to bring
But cold intelligence of death upon my tides of
Spring?

Now grief is in my shadow, and it seems well enough
To be there with my fathers, where neither fear nor
love
Can touch me more, nor spite of men, nor my own
teasing blame,
While the slow mosses weave an end of my forgotten
name.

CLIFFORD DYMENT

46. *Glory*

WHEN you were speaking I was not with you,
I heard none of the words you said;
I was translated from
My sensible head.

I was a giant, drunk
With the ichor of every vine;

I set fire to the Australian bush—
My brand was a mountain pine.

Men were assembled in Parliament :
I kicked the building over ;
I gave the Brooklyn bridge a shake,
And it fell into the river.

By dipping in my little finger
I could make an ocean boil ;
In my palm, the iron warship
Had the charm of crinkled foil.

I was happy, squeezing crowds
To suffocation with my hand :
I was the thunder in the storm,
The havoc in the bombed land.

Loitering on Ludgate Hill
I shut St. Paul's up like a book :
I laughed so loud at this huge jest
That continents shook.

47. *A Christmas Poem*

I SEE him burning in a flame
White as a narcissus
Upon the pointed tree with silver lights
In the jolly house.

I hear him in the bells that peal
In the square stone tower,
And in the winter atmosphere
He crackles like hoar.

You who laugh and dance in brilliance,
   And you who dream of wealth,
And you, the solemn-eyed, who grieve
   For the world's thin faith,

Come, for he comes, he who burns, rings
   In bells ; he who knew well
A child's curls, and the sun-flushed rose,
   And the icicle.

48. *Fox*

EXPLOITER of the shadows
   He moved among the fences,
A strip of action coiling
Around his farmyard fancies.

With shouting fields are shaken,
The spinneys give no shelter ;
There is delight for riders,
For hounds a tooth in shoulder.

The creature tense with wildness
Knows death is sudden falling
From fury into weary
Surrendering of feeling.

RICHARD EBERHART

49. *The Groundhog*

IN June, amid the golden fields,
   I saw a groundhog lying dead.

Dead lay he ; my senses shook,
And mind outshot our naked frailty.
There lowly in the vigorous summer
His form began its senseless change,
And made my senses waver dim
Seeing nature ferocious in him.
Inspecting close his maggot's might
And seething cauldron of his being,
Half with loathing, half with a strange love,
I poked him with an angry stick.
The fever arose, became a flame
And Vigour circumscribed the skies,
Immense energy in the sun,
And through my frame a sunless trembling.
My stick had done nor good nor harm.
Then stood I silent in the day
Watching the object, as before ;
And kept my reverence for knowledge
Trying for control, to be still,
To quell the passion of the blood ;
Until I had bent down on my knees
Praying for joy in the sight of decay
And so I left ; and I returned
In Autumn strict of eye, to see
The sap gone out of the groundhog,
But the bony sodden hulk remained.
But the year had lost its meaning,
And in intellectual chains
I lost both love and loathing,
Mured up in the wall of wisdom.
Another summer took the fields again
Massive and burning, full of life,
But when I chanced upon the spot

RICHARD EBERHART

There was only a little hair left,
And bones bleaching in the sunlight
Beautiful as architecture ;
I watched them like a geometer,
And cut a walking stick from a birch.
It has been three years, now.
There is no sign of the groundhog.
I stood there in the whirling summer,
My hand capped a withered heart,
And thought of China and of Greece,
Of Alexander in his tent ;
Of Montaigne in his tower,
Of Saint Theresa in her wild lament.

ROBIN FLOWER

50. *Personality*

YOU have not been before
  And will not be again,
Not just that confident glance and spirit sure
  Nor cheek of just that grain,
Your stillness like checked speed,
  Your going like a spear,
Quick eyes and swift voice instant to the need
  And light laugh crystal-clear.

These things not Helen owned,
  Not she of Egypt, nor
That loveliness that the wise people stoned
  Lest it should bring them war,
Not whatsoe'er was sweet
  In the world's spring, or when

ROBIN FLOWER

Summer and arduous autumn made complete
    All beauty among men.

And if before the end
    All lovely things were brought,
All perilous dreams great spirits had to friend
    Too high for human thought,
All the witched world found rare,
    All fire, all light, all dew,
All stars inhabiting the heavenly air—
    They would not make up you.

For still behind these things
    That are but as your dress
You hide in you and from your spirit's springs
    Feed that high loveliness,
Which having wrought, the gods
    Go sorrowing for Time's sake,
Who makes and in his hurrying periods
    Must all things made unmake.

JOHN FREEMAN

51. *The Ship*

WAS that a sound?
    If sound it was, 'tis gone:
Silence returns all round,

As if a star had shone
A moment from the black;
Or a white bird on

JOHN FREEMAN

Dark waves, then back
Past sight had flown
With flying scud and rack.

It was a sound
Singing very near,
Whispering all round,

Dying on the ear :
It was the wind
Thin and clear

Running behind,
Then somewhere overhead
Moving like one blind

That feels his way
In the gentle dark
Of night and day.

Between the wires stark
The wind stirred :
Hark, hark !

Gone—as a bird
Half seen, unknown.
Our ears heard,

And the sound has flown.
But the listening mind
Trembles on . . . on.

JOHN FREEMAN

52. *The Centaurs*

THE silken horses chafe and shift
Under the falling chestnut petals,
Tossing aloft cream-foamy crests,
A fine rain slants, the blown dust settles.

The silken horses leap at last,
Are curbed, released, re-curbed, requickened :
Like swift rain slanted from the hills
Or thin beams before clouds have thickened

They flow down the hill's flowing breast.
Leap now the horses into meadows,
Through waves of grasses plunge and slide
Bearing their riders light as shadows.

The riders with the heaving shapes
Inblent wade through the grassy surges
In centaur-wise, lift glittering eyes
Nearing the salt sea's hoary marges.

The salt sea blossoms whiter fall,
Wilder the waves of the salt sea meadows.
Horses and horsemen centaur-wise
Plunge and vanish sudden as shadows.

JOHN GAWSWORTH

53. *Roman Headstone*

JULIA, *carissima Julia,*
Strange how you hold a beauty for me now
As though no sixteen centuries had dimmed your
charm,
And only crusted stones remained to trace
Your exile life, here where I seek not balm
To heal such wounds of body as once scarred your lord,
But silence for my mind and peace for hands
That they may cease their restless artifice
And stretch at ease in tendrils and grass strands!

Julia, carissima Julia,
Strange that no woman bears the likeness now
That you have set upon my tablet mind,
Not in obliterated text as here
In perpetuum ave carved I find,
A valediction lichenised and broken!
Beyond what ultimate are you? I ponder.
In perpetuum ave atque vale.

Julia, where do you wander?

54. *The Mill*

TURVILLE Mill is broken,
The fabric starkly rent;
Yet stands it to betoken
Decay's slow argument.

JOHN GAWSWORTH

In wind-blown dereliction
  The shaking antic spars
Creak their last malediction
  Against the eternal stars.

WILFRID GIBSON

55. *The Hood-Seals*

THE ice-blink quivered in the sky : I smelt
  The smell of ice, and in my marrow felt
The chill of the floe's approaching days before
We set out, sealing, from the Island shore,
First of the wooden-walls that sealing-spring
Out from the harbour of St. John's, to bring
In hulls of oak and greenheart a rich spoil
Of harp and hood sculps, fat with blubber oil :
And when we sailed the ice was still unseen
Even from the truck-slung barrel where the keen
Eyes of the scunner strained for the first sight
Of the southward-drifting icefield, vast and white,
That brought to us our harvest of hair-seal.

And so, day after day, with thrusting keel
The ship bore north through buffeting short seas
That sluiced the decks, till spray began to freeze
Our beards to glass, and stiffen stay and shroud
With ice one night as, under driving cloud
That, blinding, baffled the chink-seeking moon,
We steamed : but dawn came, clear-horizoned, and
  soon

The masthead-lookout gave the welcome cry—
" Ice ! Ice ! "—and every northward-staring eye
Glimpsed glimmering level and glittering hummock
and spire
Kindling already in the dawn's red fire.
And then from nowhere fog swirled suddenly
Like giant swathes of gossamer over the sea ;
And with the fog the snow came, hard and dry,
Driving down on us from the unseen sky.
Yet still we battled slowly towards the floe
Through mist and blizzard, cloaked with clogging snow,
Northward and ever northward till we felt
The steel-shod cutwater crash into a belt
Of rafting pans and growlers ; and so knew
We neared the whelping-ice we must cut through,
The stout ship standing up to strain and stress,
Till we should reach its innermost recess,
The secret white heart, whose security
From shark and narwal or prowling enemy
The timid harp-seals seek year after year,
Trusting in peace their tender young to rear,
The blubber-padded whitecoats who supply
The richest oil for soap, and so must die !

Day after day through that ice-cluttered sea
We steamed through flurry and smother steadily ;
And, as we pushed on blindly, we could feel
Half-sunken growlers gride along the keel
And slob-ice graze the beam and butt the bow
That crunched through bobbing hunks and chunks
that now
Closed on us, crowding and jostling ; and then the snow
Stopped suddenly ; and we saw the great main floe

Right on us ; and the fog began to clear
So we could take our bearings and then steer
For a free channel through the mounded ice
Into its heart where, gripped, as in a vice,
By the main-ridge pressure, our wooden walls might
  crush
Like matchboard on us. So, through sish and slush
And slob we steamed 'twixt ice-walls, till at last
A hummock barred our passage and jammed us fast
As the cut froze in astern. We leapt to the floe
With poles, ice-saws and chisels ; and, numb and slow,
We cut and thrust and tugged, with a hawser lashed
To the bollards, till the hummock in splinters crashed
About the butting bow ; and free again
We sailed awhile until we thrust in vain
Against a huger hummock that blocked our course,
For all our butting and cutting ; and we'd to force
And blast our way through it with dynamite.

So, on into the floe by day and night,
Butting and blasting, in blizzard and fog and bright
White blinding spells of sunshine, we pierced our way
Until at last at the red end of a day
Of crazing killing cold we grinned to see
That we had reached the harp-seal rookery,
The crowded main-patch upon which we burst
Through a great hummock, proud to get there first.

And on that waste of whelping-ice all night
'Neath shivering spears and quivering crowns of light,
Purple and green, and sweeping swords of white
Where the aurora blazing over us hung,
The barking harp-seals and their bawling young

Kept up a clamour ; and I could not sleep,
But sought the deck again and again, to peep
At the silly scrambling puppies playing there
So happily under that fantastic flare ;
And watched them from the glassy deck alone
Until the cold, icing me to the bone,
Drove me below . . .
At glint of dawn began
The slaughter of the innocents, each man,
As in a frenzy of murder, clubbing dead
The plump whitecoats whose frightened parents fled,
Showing no fight, just scrambling frantically
Before us, flapping and barking helplessly.

And I, too, young and heedless and half-crazed
With cold and that nightmare passage, ran and raised
My gaff to strike ; and saw black baby eyes
Looking up at me, fearless, with no surprise
In their dark stare . . . I struck . . . then heard a shout . . .
And, dizzy and half-sick, I turned about,
To see my messmates, running before a herd
Of the huge fighting hoods that, anger-stirred
By the slaughter, from behind a hummock surged,
Through fellow-feeling for their seal-kind urged
To the rescue of the timid harps . . .
Astare
I stood and waited, stunned and frozen there :
And a great bull was on me in a trice
Roaring . . . I struck at him . . . slipped on the ice . . .
And knew no more . . .
Though, seemingly, the ship
Was nipped and crushed to touchwood in the grip

Of suddenly-rafting ice . . . at least no more
Was heard of her . . . and it seems my comrades bore
My senseless body back across the floe,
Struggling and blundering through the baffling snow,
Till, one by one, done in by cold, they fell
In fatal frost-sleep on that field of hell . . .
Yet I, though how, it seems I'll never know,
Was rescued from the death-trap of the floe . . .
Happen another ship's crew . . .
But the fear
Of that huge hood-seal lunging—though quite clear
I can recall each instant of that dread
Hell-passage into the ice—strikes my heart dead,
Again and yet again, when I would think . . .
Striving to take a hold on life, I sink
Under that ferocious onslaught . . .
And, night and day,
Retracing and retracing its blind way
Through fog and blizzard, my numb soul struggles, until
I stand once more with gaff upraised to kill . . .

56. *Out of the Air*

NO song-bird will ever
Come to my call ;
But when I am thinking
Of nothing at all,
Thinking of nothing
And going nowhere,
Out of the air
The crystal notes fall.

LORD GORELL

57. *The Coat*

I

IT was the evening of an awesome day.
The sun sank early into blood-red wrath ;
Darkness came ravening ; tempests arose,
Hungrily howling, and the path
Of every traveller beset like birds of prey :
Great rocks were shattered as with giants' blows ;
Earth shook ; from cloud-banks streamed the rain :
No concord was there in the world but pain.

II

Dismissed from duty, straight the soldier went,
Buffeting his way, his spoil beneath his arm,
To visit one that in an alien land
Round his rough heart had twined a charm.
As to his goal he strode, indifferent
That murmuring, frightened crowds his passage
scanned,
His thoughts, as all that day, were turned
To one sick child whose friendship he had earned.

III

Anxious he was, yet unfamiliar peace
Walked strangely with him through the streets of
storm :
He clutched its comfort as his steps drew nigh.
The mother breathed, " Welcome thy form !

He hath been crying for thee, hath no ease
Without thee, and even now is like to die ! "
With twofold pang his heart gave heed,
Sweet to be needed, bitter such the need.

IV

The child's face flushed to feel his playmate there
Touching his hand with awkward tenderness.
" Ah me," the mother sighed, " but he is cold ! "
" The gods, then, this day's labour bless,"
The soldier cried ; " that ill I can repair ! "
He grasped his bundle and a coat unrolled.
" See what I have for thee ! " he smiled,
And wrapped it gently round the dying child.

V

The storm had ended : as the soldier came
It ceased as if his hand had closed the door
On all but Love. Within a silent room
They watched a sleeping child : no more
Their eyes were wan upon a wasted frame ;
They saw in wonder all his childhood bloom.
" The coat has snatched him from the dead !
See how he sleeps ! " the mother, marvelling, said.

VI

" His lips are pressed against it, and his hands
Clutch at its folds as he had found a friend
To gather to his very heart : it seems
Almost as though his ears attend
Upon an unseen healer who commands

The fever halt and turn to tranquil dreams !
Dost thou not also mark the change ?
Whence hast thou brought this coat ? 'Tis passing
strange ! "

VII

" By lucky cast I won it : I have been,"
The soldier answered, " on that stark hillside
Holding the rabble, keeping watch all day
Upon three felons crucified.
This was the coat of one, a Nazarene ;
A righteous man, I heard the captain say :
I know not that ; I took no note—
But may the gods receive him for his coat ! "

C. L. GRAVES

58. *To Goya*

(1746–1828)

GOYA, sprung from stock plebeian,
homely-featured, yet with gifts and claims
Making you a Royal minion,
friend and more than friend of noble dames.

Brawler, anarch, opportunist—
never was a stranger medley known—
Venting your satiric frenzy
in the very shadow of the Throne.

C. L. GRAVES

Gloating with a ghoul-like fancy
on the stricken field where vultures feast,
Or the underworld exploring
to reveal the naked human beast.

Horror you pursued and beauty,
till you had outlived the Psalmist's span,
With an industry prodigious
as your wild ungodly race you ran.

In your heart you were a rebel,
yet, when thrones and sceptres tumbled down,
Served with an impartial homage
those who wore or lost or filched the Crown.

Of your brood of twenty children
all but one in early childhood died,
Yet your name and fame have flourished
and the canker of the years defied.

Still mid other famous trophies
in the halls of Strathfieldsaye we view
Records of your stormy meetings
with the man who won at Waterloo—

Wellington, whose haughty manners
you, 'tis said, once threatened to chastise,
Though in truth no other artist
painted him in more heroic guise.

Still beside the great Velasquez
uneclipsed your masterpieces shine,
Steeped in an unearthly glamour
that is neither human nor divine ;

C. L. GRAVES

Still enshrined within the Prado
  in your glowing canvases remain
All the havoc and the splendour,
  all the charm and devilry of Spain.

I. SUTHERLAND GROOM

59. *Daughter of Jephthah*

TRIUMPHING, home he came,
  Charioted in a hero's name,
  The news, fire-spurred,
  Aroused the light-slept huntsman and goatherd,
The very valley
Chanted the praise of him and his war rally:
  Forgotten now
  The passionate rash vow,
The heaven-heard
Inviolable word
  Pledging the first to greet him to the slaughter,—
  Till, in reluctant dawn behold—his daughter!

(Ah, had he but foreseen
The dancing girls, foreknown the tambourine,
Forethought the waking when the dawn was
    dim,
The new dance steps rehearsed to welcome
    him!

I. SUTHERLAND GROOM

The dance, he knew,
Sprang from his daughter, growing as she grew,
But the wild tune
Was old as balm, old as the Gilead moon.)

A word, and all was over :
Even the sullen hillside drover
Watching afar,
Saw the eclipse of Jephthah's triumph star,
And knew the token
Of the fell oath though little had been spoken :
But for two moons,
—Most pitiful of boons—
Meadow and valley,
Firred summit and oak alley
The daughter due for sacrifice was free
To roam unfettered in sweet company.

The Gilead hills were fair,
The terebinth and balsam there,
The prickly oak
Wove in the heat a green impervious cloak,
The dawn slow stealing
Over the hills brought more than balm for healing,
The woods of pine
In shadow and sunshine,
Terebinth shade,
And oleander glade,
These, and the goats' bleat and the goodly sky
And mountain waters taught her how to die.

I. SUTHERLAND GROOM

Spectres of wayward moons
Glancing askance at midnight noons
    Surprise a throng
    Of Gilead ghosts chanting a Gilead song
By mountain water
About the slender ghost of Jephthah's daughter :
    There the stars hear
    Lyrical sounds and clear,
The shaken timbrel,
The noted pipe and cymbal,
    Throughout the summer nights on hills balm-clad
    Rising above the plains of Gilead.

THOMAS HARDY

60. *Weathers*

I

THIS is the weather the cuckoo likes,
    And so do I ;
When showers betumble the chestnut spikes,
    And nestlings fly :
And the little brown nightingale bills his best,
And they sit outside at " The Travellers' Rest,"
And maids come forth sprig-muslin drest,
And citizens dream of the south and west,
    And so do I.

II

This is the weather the shepherd shuns,
    And so do I ;

When beeches drip in browns and duns,
    And thresh, and ply ;
And hill-hid tides throb, throe on throe,
And meadow rivulets overflow,
And drops on gate-bars hang in a row,
And rooks in families homeward go,
    And so do I.

61. *We Field-Women*

HOW it rained
    When we worked at Flintcomb-Ash,
And could not stand upon the hill
Trimming swedes for the slicing-mill.
The wet washed through us—plash, plash, plash :
    How it rained !

    How it snowed
When we crossed from Flintcomb-Ash
To the Great Barn for drawing reed,
Since we could nowise chop a swede.—
Flakes in each doorway and casement-sash :
    How it snowed !

    How it shone
When we went from Flintcomb-Ash
To start at dairywork once more
In the laughing meads, with cows three-score,
And pails, and songs, and love—too rash :
    How it shone !

62. *He never Expected Much*

[or]

A Consideration [A Reflection] on my Eighty-sixth Birthday

WELL, World, you have kept faith with me,
  Kept faith with me;
Upon the whole you have proved to be
  Much as you said you were.
Since as a child I used to lie
Upon the leaze and watch the sky,
Never, I own, expected I
  That life would all be fair.

'Twas then you said, and since have said,
  Times since have said,
In that mysterious voice you shed
  From clouds and hills around:
"Many have loved me desperately,
Many with smooth serenity,
While some have shown contempt of me
  Till they dropped underground.

"I do not promise overmuch,
  Child; overmuch;
Just neutral-tinted haps and such,"
  You said to minds like mine.
Wise warning for your credit's sake!
Which I for one failed not to take,
And hence could stem such strain and ache
  As each year might assign.

63. *The Carpenter*

SILENT at Joseph's side He stood,
And smoothed and trimmed the shapeless wood,
And with firm hand, assured and slow,
Drove in each nail with measured blow.

Absorbed, He planned a wooden cask,
Nor asked for any greater task,
Content to make, with humble tools,
Tables and little children's stools.

Lord, give me careful hands to make
Such simple things as for Thy sake,
Happy within Thine house to dwell
If I may make one table well.

64. *The Dancer*

WHEN this body, that I have schooled to interpret
Each sound in motion effortless and sure,
That rises to a pinnacle of silence,
Seeming to pause an instant there, secure,
Shall at the last fall from a wide-flung gesture
Into the cold rigidity of death,
And lie so heavily, that once was lighter
Than thistledown that veers to every breath,
Lay me not then in the dark earth unfriendly,
Where never leaf shall sway nor flower nod,

And I shall slowly sink into corruption
Under the grass my dancing feet have trod.

Take me, before my limbs are set in rigor,
To a tall funeral pyre on some dark night,
Where fire eats quickly through the crackling wood
As if my speed had set the stage alight,
And flames leap up like draperies that catch
Their changing colours from the spotlight's glare—
But never dance was swift as this that makes me
One with the smoke that fades upon the air,
A handful of ashes curtseying in the wind
On tiptoe in some strange fantastic measure ;
For so in death I dance to please myself
That gave my life to dance for others' pleasure.

CHRISTOPHER HASSALL

65. *A Country Parson is Thankful for Spring*
(A Soliloquy)

THERE is a forest all of ebony
that grows beneath the shining of the stars :
no other tree, not the imperious oak,
nor sycamore, nor plane of naked bark,
nor winter-thriving pine, may there find place,
for all are exiled by the jealousy
of that one ravenous multiplying bough.
The silent showering of atom stars
makes great the Earth, and twelve moon-footed hours
witness the increase of those leafy seeds

and their quick-withering prime. Meek Innocence
lies dreaming there, while under murderous fogs
burrows the sinning thief,—for it is Night,
hush'd period of the gem-eyed owl, wherein,
beneath the idle and the covering moon,
all through the hard frost season, God prepares
the sweet familiar miracle of Spring.
And now I wake, and it is in the air ;
and now I wake, and on the sparkling grass
there lies a sheen as of a freezing fire.
Earth has achieved, has bent the frosty bar,
and the long icicled hours relent and thaw.
How shyly do the hedges mention Spring
with brown-assembling buds, sure warrant of
the Lord's continuing good ! While near and far,
because of mildness in the sky, the clay
gives forth a new unspotted world, whose shoots
and frail bloom-promises as yet are strange
to the night-visiting beetle. This new dawn
reveals a world too blameless and too young
for blight and rottenness, a lust of life
too fierce to realise the soon approach
and watchfulness of winter. Must this time,
this crystalline and nimble time, which now
is cradled in the air, not last for ever,
not scape the yellowing leaf and sharp attack
of disappointing winds ? O how the scent
of freshness and revolving sap mounts up,
triumphs at every turn, spreads with the sun,
pleasing the season's heart ! This shall inspire
my secret prayer, that the reviving life
within my soul, this sympathy with Nature,
remain for ever perfect ; though the winds

chase the red leaf across the weir, and snap
the crisp twig from the beech, and all the sky
mourns in deep funeral black, this youngling ray
of morning and the new-conceived year
shall glitter in my thought. Let everything
be thankful ; my parishioners, even those,
lost in the unidentifying soil,
whose place is vacant at the holy rail,
who bide the late alarm, let them praise God,
musing His worship while the quick bring songs.
The dead are with us closer in the Spring ;
though their frail bodies are but shapes of mist
distill'd out of the ground, and their dry tongues
softer in operation than the breeze
puff'd on the matins leaf, who feels them not ?
Their voices weave the colour of the grass,
their strength is in the fervour of the earth.
Daylight and darkness, let all things conspire
to honour Him, man, beast, and this glad county,
this heaven-favoured shire, hallowed with lanes
and smoking cottages inhabited
by simple love ; especially the Weald,
lying so unrebellious, so serene,
under the sway of the long-shoulder'd downs,
her drowsy nooks and sun-rebuffing trees,
obedient sheep together with the herds
that crop the grass, the dew-ponds where they drink,
their shelters, and their grazings, and their folds.
Earth has achieved !
What glad approach ! What festival of buds !
Renewal of music in the eaves, return
of the unboastful primrose, watery-eyed,
and all the tender thrustings from the ground,

because of Summer breathing in his tomb,
because of an old promise once again
most beautifully brought to pass, by Him
whose hand is on the forehead of the world!

66. *To the Australian Eucalyptus*

SOCIABLE, tremendous tree,
how exquisitely pattern'd! With what grace
your tall form sways, as to a tune,
leaves dance, twigs interlace
with a sweet trouble, so companionable to me!

Very beautiful, long tree,
though every side your lovely cousins crowd
in tapering prime, they must not fret
that I should be allowed
to court you with a sonnet, individually;

for you must share it, tree,
just as you do the varied earth and air,
since all alike, with sister grace
and family pride, you wear
smooth lady-limbs of bark, rust-red and silvery.

And I have never seen
a sight of such contentment; though your leaves
are dumb, it is not hard to tell
no earthly influence grieves
the spirit of that rich unwinterable green.

Now springs that envious pain
of old remorse, continual regret—

How many of you cluster here
in company, and yet,
so different from men, in harmony remain!

O how can I transform
the wealth of your material finery
to treasure of the soul? What Spring
has fed you, giant tree,
that you so lord the earth, regardless of the storm?

O lead me to the mine
where such rare stone abounds, for I would share it,
just as you share my song. I'll risk
the world, only to wear it,
not on my outer boughs, but in my heart's deep shrine.

67. *The Arrow*

IN the forest of the air,
Jesus, with his quiver bare,
came upon a sturdy tree,
lopt a branch, and it was me.

At one end he fix'd a head
barb'd, and dipt in venom red,
venom that could raise the dead,
life-blood for my Safety shed.

Then he split the arrow through,
gave it speed with feathers two;
nick'd and finish'd, I was stor'd
in the quiver of the Lord.

Presently he spied the foe,
strung me ready in his bow ;
still I fly, and still I fly,
flying till the day I die :

speed he gave me, and good aim ;
may I, in my Maker's name,
never use it to his shame,
never from the purpose slip

of his master-marksmanship,
never, never cease to try,
that if the arrow fall awry
none may blame his Archery.

A. P. HERBERT

68. *My Ship*

MY ship is my delight,
  And she's the one I woo
When in the shiny night
  We dance across the blue,
With whispering sail and spar
As live as ladies are,
  And twenty times as true.

My ship is my delight,
  I made her, she is mine,
I built her trim and tight,
  I dreamed her gracious line ;

A. P. HERBERT

No wooden thing is she
But some proud part of me;
I made her, she is mine.

Then at the helm I stand
And not alone are we.
Two lovers, hand in hand,
We ask no company.
So, by some lover's art
I think she knows my heart
And sings or sighs with me.

GERARD MANLEY HOPKINS

69. *The Windhover:*
to Christ our Lord

I CAUGHT this morning morning's minion, king-
dom of daylight's dauphin, dapple-dawn-drawn Falcon, in his riding
Of the rolling level underneath him steady air, and
striding
High there, how he rung upon the rein of a wimpling
wing
In his ecstasy! then off, off forth on swing,
As a skate's heel sweeps smooth on a bow-bend:
the hurl and gliding
Rebuffed the big wind. My heart in hiding
Stirred for a bird,—the achieve of, the mastery of the
thing!

Brute beauty and valour and act, oh, air, pride, plume,
here
Buckle! AND the fire that breaks from thee then,
a billion
Times told lovelier, more dangerous, O my chevalier!

No wonder of it: shéer plód makes plough down
sillion
Shine, and blue-bleak embers, ah my dear,
Fall, gall themselves, and gash gold-vermilion.

70. *God's Grandeur*

THE world is charged with the grandeur of God.
It will flame out, like shining from shook foil;
It gathers to a greatness, like the ooze of oil
Crushed. Why do men then now not reck his rod?
Generations have trod, have trod, have trod;
And all is seared with trade; bleared, smeared with
toil;
And wears man's smudge and shares man's smell: the soil
Is bare now, nor can foot feel, being shod.

And for all this, nature is never spent;
There lives the dearest freshness deep down things;
And though the last lights off the black West went
Oh, morning, at the brown brink eastward,
springs—
Because the Holy Ghost over the bent
World broods with warm breast and with ah!
bright wings.

71. *Felix Randal*

FELIX RANDAL the farrier, O he is dead then? my duty all ended,
Who have watched his mould of man, big-boned and hardy-handsome
Pining, pining, till time when reason rambled in it and some
Fatal four disorders, fleshed there, all contended?

Sickness broke him. Impatient he cursed at first, but mended
Being anointed and all; though a heavenlier heart began some
Months earlier, since I had our sweet reprieve and ransom
Tendered to him. Ah well, God rest him all road ever he offended!

This seeing the sick endears them to us, us too it endears.
My tongue had taught thee comfort, touch had quenched thy tears,
Thy tears that touched my heart, child, Felix, poor Felix Randal;

How far from then forethought of, all thy more boisterous years,
When thou at the random grim forge, powerful amidst peers,
Didst fettle for the great grey drayhorse his bright and battering sandal!

72. *Pied Beauty*

GLORY be to God for dappled things—
For skies of couple-colour as a brinded cow ;
For rose-moles all in stipple upon trout that swim ;
Fresh-firecoal chestnut-falls ; finches' wings ;
Landscape plotted and pieced—fold, fallow, and plough ;
And áll trádes, their gear and tackle and trim.

All things counter, original, spare, strange ;
Whatever is fickle, freckled (who knows how ?)
With swift, slow ; sweet, sour ; adazzle, dim ;
He fathers-forth whose beauty is past change :
Praise him.

73. *Inversnaid*

THIS darksome burn, horseback brown,
His rollrock highroad roaring down,
In coop and in comb the fleece of his foam
Flutes and low to the lake falls home.

A windpuff-bonnet of fáwn-fróth
Turns and twindles over the broth
Of a pool so pitchblack, féll-frówning,
It rounds and rounds Despair to drowning.

Degged with dew, dappled with dew
Are the groins of the braes that the brook treads through,
Wiry heathpacks, flitches of fern,
And the beadbonny ash that sits over the burn.

What would the world be, once bereft
Of wet and of wildness? Let them be left,
O let them be left, wildness and wet;
Long live the weeds and the wilderness yet.

E. V. KNOX

74. *The Water Zoo*

TO-DAY I have seen all I wish,
For I have seen four thousand fish,
Inscrutable and rum,
Observing me with solemn eyes
That hold no anger or surprise,
In the Aquarium.

Because they float about my brain,
To-morrow I should like to come,
And see four thousand fish again.

For there are pike and trout and carp,
And fish with faces long and sharp,
And wrasse with their mosaic scales,
And oblong fish that have no tails;
Fresh-water and soft-water fellows,
And fish with valves that work like bellows;
And fish that leap and fish that crawl,
And great octopodes a-sprawl,
Inside those aqueous mysteries
Below the Mappin Terraces;
And golden fish with filmy skirts
That move like Oriental flirts,

And rainbow-coloured fish that seem
Like sunsets dipped into a stream,
And silver fish with dusky bars
That float beneath the nenuphars,
And tiny fish of Paradise,
And fish with furry backs, like mice,
And fish that lay their eggs on land
By leaping, as I understand,
And placing them on grass, but yet
Must splash about to keep them wet;
The sea-hare, which is like a slug,
The wolf-fish with an awful mug,
And sharks with faces mild and prim,
Like schoolgirls, elegantly slim—
You would not dream that underneath
That tiny mouth had all those teeth—
And humorous turtles that advance
As though in some Salome dance,
And hermit-crabs that have the sense
To use a whelk-shell residence
To walk about within the sea,
Whereon there sprouts, most luckily,
A poisonous anemone.

And there are fish that kiss and climb,
And fish that croak, though not in rhyme,
And sucking-fish that hang on rocks,
And eels that give electric shocks,
And fish that turn a rosy pink—
From sheer false modesty, I think—
And fish that, floating on the tide
Transparent, show their whole inside;
Not ray-fish these, but, should you wish,

They may be termed the X-ray fish ;
And flat fish with their eyes askew,
All buried, save those eyes, from view
Beneath the clean white sand, until
With rippling movements they ascend
To eat some portion of a friend
Thrown in by keepers from the top ;
And fish that always seem to stop
Lying in one place, dull as lead,
Although you tap quite near their head ;
And salamanders dark and dire,
And axolotls, whose desire
To be a salamander fills
Their bosom with ecstatic thrills ;
But no—the awful hand of Fate
Prevents them from that longed-for state.
For grow to be a salamander
(Though striving with uncommon candour
And patient as a nurse or aunt)
The axolotl simply can't ;
Because of his peculiar gland
He may not hope to salamand ;
His life's ambition forced to throttle,
He still remains an axolotl.
And there the crayfish or *langouste*
On craggy rocks is seen to roost. . . .

To-day I have seen all I wish,
For I have seen four thousand fish,
Inscrutable and rum,
Observing me with solemn eyes
That hold no anger or surprise,
In the Aquarium.

E. V. KNOX

Because they float about my brain,
To-morrow I should like to come
And see four thousand fish again.

D. H. LAWRENCE

75. *Piano*

SOFTLY, in the dusk, a woman is singing to me;
Taking me back down the vista of years, till I see
A child sitting under the piano, in the boom of the tingling strings
And pressing the small, poised feet of a mother who smiles as she sings.

In spite of myself, the insidious mastery of song
Betrays me back, till the heart of me weeps to belong
To the old Sunday evenings at home, with winter outside
And hymns in the cosy parlour, the tinkling piano our guide.

So now it is vain for the singer to burst into clamour
With the great black piano appassionato. The glamour
Of childish days is upon me, my manhood is cast
Down in the flood of remembrance, I weep like a child for the past.

76. *Giorno dei Morti*

ALONG the avenue of cypresses,
All in their scarlet cloaks and surplices
Of linen, go the chanting choristers,
The priests in gold and black, the villagers. . . .

And all along the path to the cemetery
The round dark heads of men crowd silently,
And black-scarved faces of womenfolk, wistfully
Watch at the banner of death, and the mystery.

And at the foot of a grave a father stands
With sunken head, and forgotten, folded hands ;
And at the foot of a grave a mother kneels
With pale shut face, nor either hears nor feels

The coming of the chanting choristers
Between the avenue of cypresses,
The silence of the many villagers,
The candle-flames beside the surplices.

77. *Baby Tortoise*

YOU know what it is to be born alone,
Baby tortoise !

The first day to heave your feet little by little from the shell,
Not yet awake,
And remain lapsed on earth,
Not quite alive.

A tiny, fragile, half-animate bean.

To open your tiny beak-mouth, that looks as if it
would never open,
Like some iron door ;
To lift the upper hawk-beak from the lower base
And reach your skinny little neck
And take your first bite at some dim bit of herbage,
Alone, small insect,
Tiny bright-eye,
Slow one.

To take your first solitary bite
And move on your slow, solitary hunt.
Your bright, dark little eye,
Your eye of a dark disturbed night,
Under its slow lid, tiny baby tortoise,
So indomitable.

No one ever heard you complain.

You draw your head forward, slowly, from your little
wimple
And set forward, slow-dragging, on your four-pinned
toes;
Rowing slowly forward.
Whither away, small bird ?
Rather like a baby working its limbs,
Except that you make slow, ageless progress
And a baby makes none.

The touch of sun excites you,
And the long ages, and the lingering chill

Make you pause to yawn,
Opening your impervious mouth,
Suddenly beak-shaped, and very wide, like some
suddenly gaping pincers ;
Soft red tongue, and hard thin gums,
Then close the wedge of your little mountain front,
Your face, baby tortoise.

Do you wonder at the world, as slowly you turn your
head in its wimple
And look with laconic, black eyes ?
Or is sleep coming over you again,
The non-life ?

You are so hard to wake.

Are you able to wonder ?
Or is it just your indomitable will and pride of the
first life
Looking round
And slowly pitching itself against the inertia
Which had seemed invincible ?

The vast inanimate,
And the fine brilliance of your so tiny eye,
Challenger.
Nay, tiny shell-bird,
What a huge vast inanimate it is, that you must row
against,
What an incalculable inertia.

Challenger,
Little Ulysses, fore-runner,

No bigger than my thumb-nail,
Buon viaggio.

All animate creation on your shoulder,
Set forth, little Titan, under your battle-shield.

The ponderous, preponderate,
Inanimate universe ;
And you are slowly moving, pioneer, you alone.

How vivid your travelling seems now, in the troubled
    sunshine,
Stoic, Ulyssean atom ;
Suddenly hasty, reckless, on high toes.

Voiceless little bird,
Resting your head half out of your wimple
In the slow dignity of your eternal pause.
Alone, with no sense of being alone,
And hence six times more solitary ;
Fulfilled of the slow passion of pitching through im-
    memorial ages
Your little round house in the midst of chaos.

Over the garden earth,
Small bird,
Over the edge of all things.
Traveller,
With your tail tucked a little on one side
Like a gentleman in a long-skirted coat.

All life carried on your shoulder,
Invincible fore-runner.

78. *Song of a Man who has Come Through*

NOT I, not I, but the wind that blows through me!
A fine wind is blowing the new direction of Time.
If only I let it bear me, carry me, if only it carry me!
If only I am sensitive, subtle, oh, delicate, a winged gift!
If only, most lovely of all, I yield myself and am borrowed
By the fine, fine wind that takes its course through the chaos of the world
Like a fine, an exquisite chisel, a wedge-blade inserted;
If only I am keen and hard like the sheer tip of a wedge
Driven by invisible blows,
The rock will split, we shall come at the wonder, we shall find the Hesperides.

Oh, for the wonder that bubbles into my soul,
I would be a good fountain, a good well-head,
Would blur no whisper, spoil no expression.

What is the knocking?
What is the knocking at the door in the night?
It is somebody wants to do us harm.

No, no, it is the three strange angels.
Admit them, admit them.

JOHN LEHMANN

79. *This Excellent Machine*

THIS excellent machine is neatly planned,
A child, a half-wit would not feel perplexed:
No chance to err, you simply press the button—
At once each cog in motion moves the next,
The whole revolves, and anything that lives
Is quickly sucked towards the running band,
Where, shot between the automatic knives,
It's guaranteed to finish dead as mutton.

This excellent machine will illustrate
The Modern World divided into nations:
So neatly planned, that if you merely tap it
The armaments will start their devastations,
And though we're for it, though we're all convinced
Some fool will press the button soon or late,
We stand and stare, expecting to be minced,—
And very few are asking, *Why not scrap it?*

F. L. LUCAS

80. *King George V—Jubilee* 1935

SINCE by the gates of school, while the rooks
croaked chorus,
Our boyhood gaily heard proclaimed a King,
Laughed as the yeomanry played at war before us—
Twenty-five years; and a world's shattering.

Five summers died, and we were no longer playing.
  Far down the steel-spiked line you met our eyes,
A horseman silent amid the bugles braying,
  Where the oldest England lies.

And memory murmured—" Caesar morituri . . ."
  And the thought came—" Before the indifferent
    sight
Of these gray barrows, scorning alike the fury
  Of the ageless winds and the whir of man's young
    flight,
Is *our* end come at length, like other nations' ?
  Rides the last English King on Salisbury Plain ? "
You sat your horse. You made us no orations,
  But we heard. And you remain—

Though throne on throne has toppled, King and Kaiser,
  While hoarse throats hooted " Long live Liberty ! "
Only to turn and trample and despise her—
  Brave world of castes and outcasts by decree !
Though the Dictators' healing hands have bettered
  The chains of older tyrants with stronger steel,
Yours yet the loyalties of men unfettered
  Who speak the thing they feel.

81. *Dead Bee inside a Window-pane*

(" Through a Glass Darkly ")

SMALL feet-folded
  All journeys done,
Softly moulded,
  Velvet one.

F. L. LUCAS

Sleep, dark eyes,
   Gossamer wing ;
Death likewise
   Has lost his sting.

Forager bold
   Pollen-proud,
Fringed with gold
   Like a sunset cloud,

Now nevermore
   Shall you glide home
To the buzzing door
   Of your honey-dome.

Brief life of toil,
   All passion missed,
Rest you, loyal
   Communist.

Poor drudge ! and yet
   How hard you fought
With this magic net
   Where your wings were caught !

With this power unknown
   That pinned you there,
Rigid as stone,
   Limpid as air ;

A wizard wall
   No eye could see—
Immeasurable
   Perplexity !

Till hoarse with despair
You stabbed in vain
The invisible snare,
The inscrutable chain.

Lost endeavour !—
Man or bee,
We master never
Our mystery.

82. *To a Queen-Anne Mirror*

UNTROUBLED and unsullied and serene
Still, as when Marlborough fought and Anne was Queen,
You watch our mad world masquerading by,
A polished Cyclops, with your single eye,
That looked upon the light ere Pope's keen pen
Blinded poor Polyphemus once again,
Bidding the wily Grecian " swift let fall
The pointed torment on his visual ball." [1]
You nought " torments ". Olympianly at ease
Above the pageant of the centuries,
Unvexed by memory as the ficklest heart
That e'er made men a game and love an art,
You have forgot blue eyes that once gazed here
Like Dryads stooping to a sleeping mere,
And *belles dames sans merci*, whose smiling shades
Once on your silver flashed their gold brocades ;
Love-lock and Cupid's bow and beauty-spot,
Lap-dog and fan—forgot, forgot, forgot !

[1] Pope's *Odyssey*, ix.

Not mercy, but the sleep that nought will break,
These dames have found ; those Ladies of your Lake—
Gone ! Not a ripple. You alone awake,
Water of Lethe, pool of transience,
In whose clear depths the drowned soul sinks past
    sense,
Till in your timeless trance we seem to be
But the dim dreams of your eternity.

83. *The Pipe of Peace*

(A.D. 317)

THE lines of the Lords of Tartary
  Held Chin-yang as a net.
Hollow-eyed the warders kept their watch,
  Clutching the parapet,
(For the last dog was long slain and eaten,
  And the leanest rat a feast)
Straining their eyes to see dust rise
  Of succour from the east.

But over the ridges green as jade
  That rimmed the east, instead,
Like the round red shield of a battlefield
  The slow moon reared her head,
With her panther's pace and her fleshless face,
  That is older than the dead.

But facing the moon rose Lin-Kun,
  To Chin-yang tower climbed he.
No sword nor spear he bore in hand,

No magic book, no wizard's wand ;
Only the simple shepherd's pipe
Men play in Tartary.

Faint on the tower betwixt the sunset
He sat and the mounting moon,
Yet his fingers danced as merrily as maidens,
When meadows are blossom-strewn ;
With a sweetness that shivered through the silver
twilight,
Rang out the Shepherd's Tune.

And the Tartars, as they sat beside their camp fires
A-twinkle in a starry ring,
And the sentries as they shouted through the starlight,
Like wild wolves answering,
And the captains at council in the great lords' tents—
Camp-follower and King,
They heard—they were hushed—they listened,
At their hearts a sudden sting.

For the old men thought of the green grave-mounds,
Where those they had loved were laid,
And heavier, suddenly, on their hearts
It seemed their harness weighed ;
And the young saw again the bright, sad eyes
That had watched them ride away,
And endless ages seemed the months
Since here their leaguer lay ;
And the very curs pricked ragged ears
To hear once more the strain
That calls the Tartar flocks to fold
Through the dusk of the Tartar plain ;

So the host remembered, man by man,
  The wild waste skies of Turkestan.

That night it seemed to the watchers on the wall,
  Through the dark a river flowed ;
Till silence fell with the failing night,
  As the city's last cock crowed ;
Slowly the white stars died away ;
  Forsaken, the camp fires smouldered grey ;
And like a last waggon the round moon lay
  Far down the westward road.

LOUIS MACNEICE

84. *Song*

THE sunlight on the garden
  Hardens and grows cold,
We cannot cage the minute
Within its nets of gold ;
When all is told
We cannot beg for pardon.

Our freedom as free lances
Advances towards its end ;
The earth compels, upon it
Sonnets and birds descend ;
And soon, my friend,
We shall have no time for dances.

The sky was good for flying
Defying the church bells
And every evil iron
Siren and what it tells:
The earth compels,
We are dying, Egypt, dying

And not expecting pardon,
Hardened in heart anew,
But glad to have sat under
Thunder and rain with you,
And grateful too
For sunlight on the garden.

85. *Riding in Cars*

RIDING in cars
  On tilting roads
We have left behind
  Our household gods,
We have left behind
  The cautious clause,
The laws of the over-
  rational mind.

Frost on the window,
  Skater's figures,
Gunmen fingering
  Anxious triggers,
Stocks and shares
  (The ribbon of the rich),

The favourite down
  At the blind ditch.

Forgotten now
  The early days,
Youth's idyllic
  And dawdling ways ;
Cruising along
  On the long road
We do not notice
  The limping god.

Swinging between
  Crutches he comes
To an overture
  Of buried drums ;
His eyes will turn
  Our hands to stone,
His name is Time,
  He walks alone.

86. *Iceland*

NO shields now
  Cross the knoll,
The hills are dull
  With leaden shale,
Whose arms could squeeze
  The breath from time
And the climb is long
  From cairn to cairn.

Houses are few
  But decorous

LOUIS MACNEICE

In a ruined land
   Of sphagnum moss ;
Corrugated iron
   Farms inherit
The spirit and phrase
   Of ancient sagas.

Men have forgotten
   Anger and ambush,
To make ends meet
   Their only business :
The lover riding
   In the lonely dale
Hears the plover's
   Single pipe

And feels perhaps
   But undefined
The drift of death
   In the sombre wind
Deflating the trim
   Balloon of lust
In a grey storm
   Of dust and grit.

So we who have come
   As trippers North
Have minds no match
   For this land's girth ;
The glacier's licking
   Tongues deride

LOUIS MACNEICE

Our pride of life,
   Our flashy songs.

But the people themselves
   Who live here
Ignore the brooding
   Fear, the sphinx ;
And the radio
   With tags of tune
Defies their pillared
   Basalt crags.

Whose ancestors
   Thought that at last
The end would come
   To a blast of horns
And gods would face
   The worst in fight,
Vanish in the night
   The last, the first

Night which began
   Without device
In ice and rocks,
   No shade or shape ;
Grass and blood,
   The strife of life,
Were an interlude
   Which soon must pass

And all go back
   Relapse to rock

Under the shawl
  Of the ice-caps,
The cape which night
  Will spread to cover
The world when the living
  Flags are furled.

87. *Now that the Shapes of Mist*

NOW that the shapes of mist like hooded beggar-children
Slink quickly along the middle of the road
And the lamps draw trails of milk in ponds of lustrous lead
I am decidedly pleased not to be dead.

Or when wet roads at night reflect the clutching
Importunate fingers of trees and windy shadows
Lunge and flounce on the windscreen as I drive
I am glad of the accident of being alive.

There are so many nights with stars or close-
ly interleaved with battleship-grey or plum,
So many visitors whose Buddha-like palms are pressed
Against the windowpanes where people take their rest.

Whose favour now is yours to screen your sleep—
You need not hear the strings that are tuning for the dawn—
Mingling, my dear, your breath with the quiet breath
Of Sleep whom the old writers called the brother of Death.

88. *At Watch*

HARK, the horizon-concealed hives murmuring
Death song and life song, in whose hushed pauses
When the waste wind halts on the seas, rolling
Under the changeable mankind-covering clouds,
The Roman ages and changes of fame's note
Fill the air with awe ; in such a breathing moment
The calm echoes the names of dying kings
Or cloudy gladiators of the revolving ocean.
There is no secret kept from silent things
Absorbing, mast or tree, all thought and talk that
float
Mutably among the air-waves ; they're like the causes
Of human destiny, remaining still, upstanding
In their own perfection, lacking completely motion
They stand, they watch : below, the crowds
Move towards home, the sky withholding comment,
The earth being steadfast, the seas still rolling.

89. *Solar Creation*

THE sun, of whose terrain we creatures are,
Is the director of all human love,
Unit of time, and circle round the earth

And we are the commotion born of love
And slanted rays of that illustrious star
Peregrine of the crowded fields of birth,

The crowded lanes, the market and the tower
Like sight in pictures, real at remove,
Such is our motion on dimensional earth.

Down by the river, where the ragged are,
Continuous the cries and noise of birth,
While to the muddy edge dark fishes move

And over all, like death, or sloping hill,
Is nature, which is larger and more still.

90. *Fortune*

THE natural silence of a tree
The motion of a mast upon the fresh-tossing sea
Now foam-inclined, now to the sun with dignity

Or the stone brow of a mountain
Regarded from a town, or the curvet fountain
Or one street-stopped in wonder at the fountain

Or a great cloud entering the room of the sky
Napoleon of his century
Heard come to knowing music consciously

Such, not us, reflect and have their day
We are but vapour of today
Unless love's chance fall on us and call us away

As the wind takes what it can
And blowing on the fortunate face, reveals the man.

91. *Wood-Pigeons*

OFTEN the woodman scares them as he comes
Swinging his axe to split the fallen birch:
The keeper with his nim-nosed dog at search
Flushes them unaware; then the hive hums.

Then from the sheddings underneath the beech,
Where squirrels rout, the flock of pigeons goes,
Their wings like sticks in battle giving blows,
The hundred hurtling to be out of reach.

Their wings flash white above a darker fan,
In drifts the colour of the smoke they pass,
They disappear above the valley grass,
They re-appear against the woodland tan.

Now that the valley woodlands are all bare,
Their flocks drift daily thus, now up, now down,
Blue-grey against the sodden of the brown,
Grey-blue against the twig-tips, thin in air.

It is a beauty none but autumn has,
These drifts of blue-grey birds whom Nature binds
Into communities of single minds,
From early leaf-fall until Candlemas.

So in the failing Life when Death and Dread,
With axe and mongrel, stalk the withering wood,
The pigeons of the spirit's solitude
Clatter to glory at the stealthy tread,

And, each made deathless by the Spirit's joy,
Launch from the leaves that have forgotten green,
And from the valley seek another scene,
That Dread can darken not, nor Death destroy.

HUW MENAI

92. *Row Leisurely*

ROW leisurely thy little boat
  And whistle on thy way,
Pausing for prayer or else to note
  The wonder of each day.

Warm thy hands by the inward sun,
  Know ghost of hope for guide—
A phosphorescent ripple on
  The world's dark sinister tide!

Follow thou not the fool my boy
  Who strives to put so bold
More living into life, more joy
  Or work than it will hold.

Know Vanity for a sickly weed;
  The power of wealth despise,
When only a penny Death will need
  To close thy sightless eyes.

Broods not the shadow of the End
  E'er here where none shall know

The reason why we came my friend
  Or whether we shall go

Beyond the grave, which none shall miss,
  Mute master of all strife,
Where lost the key of wedlock is
  And husband knows not wife,

Nor mother child, nor father son,
  Where dust is love and pride,
Where they shall never more be one
  Though sleeping side by side?

Row leisurely thy boat dear lad,
  The harbour's e'er in view,
And thou shalt surely reach it, glad
  To sleep the long night through!

E. H. W. MEYERSTEIN

93. *A Sundial*

I NUMBER none but hours serene;
  The days are mine, but not the nights;
Over my dark-lined visage lean
Children, amid their summer rites,
Chasing the shadow every way,
Till butterflies distract their play.

A pillar lifts me up to meet
The moving message of the sun;

My gnomon tires not ; I regreet
The dewless motes that slide and run.
I share no Phaethon's fatal zeal ;
Heaven strikes, but sunders not, my wheel.

I shall remain when both are dead
Who placed me in this walk of box,
Long after their last bloom is shed
By the sweet-william and the phlox.
Eternity I may not boast,
Yet I wear out more time than most.

HAROLD MONRO

94. *The Ocean in London*

IN London while I slowly wake
At morning I'm amazed to hear
The ocean, seventy miles away,
Below my window roaring, near.

When first I know that heavy sound
I keep my eyelids closely down,
And sniff the brine, and hold all thought
Reined back outside the walls of town.

So I can hardly well believe
That those tremendous billows are
Of iron and steel and wood and glass :
Van, lorry, and gigantic car.

95. *Midnight Lamentation*

WHEN you and I go down
Breathless and cold,
Our faces both worn back
To earthly mould,
How lonely we shall be!
What shall we do,
You without me,
I without you?

I cannot bear the thought
You, first, may die,
Nor of how you will weep,
Should I.
We are too much alone;
What can we do
To make our bodies one:
You, me; I, you?

We are most nearly born
Of one same kind;
We have the same delight,
The same true mind.
Must we then part, we part;
Is there no way
To keep a beating heart,
And light of day?

I could now rise and run
Through street on street
To where you are breathing—you,
That we might meet,

And that your living voice
Might sound above
Fear, and we two rejoice
Within our love.

How frail the body is,
And we are made
As only in decay
To lean and fade.
I think too much of death ;
There is a gloom
When I can't hear your breath
Calm in some room.

O, but how suddenly
Either may droop ;
Countenance be so white,
Body stoop.
Then there may be a place
Where fading flowers
Drop on a lifeless face
Through weeping hours.

Is then nothing safe ?
Can we not find
Some everlasting life
In our one mind ?
I feel it like disgrace
Only to understand
Your spirit through your word,
Or by your hand.

I cannot find a way
Through love and through ;

I cannot reach beyond
Body, to you.
When you or I must go
Down evermore,
There'll be no more to say
—But a locked door.

EDWIN MUIR

96. *Merlin*

O MERLIN in your crystal cave
Deep in the diamond of the day,
Will there ever be a singer
Whose music will smooth away
The furrow drawn by Adam's finger
Across the meadow and the wave?
Or a runner who'll outrun
Man's long shadow driving on,
Break through the gate of memory
And hang the apple on the tree?
Will your magic ever show
The sleeping bride shut in her bower,
The day wreathed in its mound of snow
And Time locked in his tower?

97. *The Threefold Place*

THIS is the place. The autumn field is bare,
The row lies half-cut all the afternoon,

The birds are hiding in the woods, the air
  Dreams fitfully outworn with waiting.
                                        Soon

Out of the russet woods in amber mail
  Heroes come walking through the yellow sheaves,
Walk on and meet. And then a silent gale
  Scatters them on the field like autumn leaves.

Yet not a feathered stalk has stirred, and all
  Is still again, but for the birds that call
On every warrior's head and breast and shield.
  Sweet cries and horror on the field.

One field. I look again and there are three:
  One where the heroes fell to rest,
One where birds make of iron limbs a tree,
  Helms for a nest,
  And one where grain stands up like armies drest.

98. *The Mountains*

THE days have closed behind my back
  Since I came into these hills.
Now memory is a single field
  One peasant tills and tills.

So far away, if I should turn
  I know I could not find
That place again. These mountains make
  The backward gaze half-blind,

Yet sharp my sight till it can catch
  The ranges rising clear
Far in futurity's high-walled land ;
  But I am rooted here.

And do not know where lies my way,
  Backward or forward. If I could
I'd leap Time's bound or turn and hide
  From Time in my ancestral wood.

Double delusion ! Here I'm held
  By the mystery of the rock,
Must watch in a perpetual dream
  The horizon's gates unlock and lock,

See on the harvest fields of Time
  The mountains heaped like sheaves,
And the valleys opening out
  Like a volume's turning leaves,

Dreaming of a peak whose height
  Will show me every hill,
A single mountain on whose side
  Life blooms for ever and is still.

SEAN O'CASEY

99. *Chorus*

From " Within the Gates "

OUR mother, the earth, is a maiden again, young, fair, and a maiden again.
Our mother, the earth, is a maiden again, young, fair, and a maiden again.

Her thoughts are a dance as she seeks out her Bride-
groom, the Sun, through the lovely confusion of
singing of birds, and of blossom and bud.
She feels the touch of his hand on her hair, on her
cheeks, in the budding of trees,
She feels the warm kiss of his love on her mouth, on
her breast, as she dances along
Through the lovely confusion of singing of birds and
of blossom and bud.
Her thoughts are a dance as she seeks out her Bride-
groom, the Sun, through the lovely confusion of
singing of birds, and of blossom and bud.
She hears the fiercely sung song of the birds, busy
building new homes in the hedge ;
She hears a challenge to life and to death as she dances
along
Through the lovely confusion of singing of birds and
of blossom and bud.
Her thoughts are a dance as she seeks out her Bride-
groom, the Sun, through the lovely confusion of
singing of birds, and of blossom and bud.
Our mother, the earth, is a maiden again, young, fair,
and a maiden again ;
Our mother, the earth, is a maiden again, she's young,
and is fair, and a maiden again !

100. *Chant of the Down-and-Outs*

From " Within the Gates "

LIFE has pass'd by us to the loud roll of her drum,
With her waving flags of yellow and green held
high,

All starr'd with golden, flaming names of her most
mighty children.

Oh, where shall we go when the day calls ?
Oh, where shall we sleep when the night falls ?
We've but a sigh for a song, and a deep sigh for a
drum-beat !

We challenge life no more, no more, with our dead
faith and our dead hope ;
We carry furled the fainting flags of a dead hope and
a dead faith.
Day sings no song, neither is there room for rest
beside night in her sleeping :
We've but a sigh for a song, and a deep sigh for a
drum-beat.

WILFRED OWEN

101. *My Shy Hand*

MY shy hand shades a hermitage apart,
O large enough for thee, and thy brief hours.
Life there is sweeter held than in God's heart,
Stiller than in the heavens of hollow flowers.

The wine is gladder there than in gold bowls.
And Time shall not drain thence, nor trouble spill.
Sources between my fingers feed all souls,
Where thou mayest cool thy lips, and draw thy fill.

Five cushions hath my hand, for reveries ;
And one deep pillow for thy brow's fatigues ;
Languor of June all winterlong, and ease
For ever from the vain untravelled leagues.

Thither your years may gather in from storm,
And Love, that sleepeth there, will keep thee warm.

102. *Insensibility*

I

HAPPY are men who yet before they are killed
Can let their veins run cold.
Whom no compassion fleers
Or makes their feet
Sore on the alleys cobbled with their brothers.
The front line withers,
But they are troops who fade, not flowers,
For poets' tearful fooling :
Men, gaps for filling :
Losses who might have fought
Longer ; but no one bothers.

II

And some cease feeling
Even themselves or for themselves.
Dullness best solves
The tease and doubt of shelling,
And Chance's strange arithmetic
Comes simpler than the reckoning of their shilling.
They keep no check on armies' decimation.

III

Happy are these who lose imagination :
They have enough to carry with ammunition.
Their spirit drags no pack,
Their old wounds save with cold can not more ache.
Having seen all things red,
Their eyes are rid
Of the hurt of the colour of blood for ever.
And terror's first constriction over,
Their hearts remain small-drawn.
Their senses in some scorching cautery of battle
Now long since ironed,
Can laugh among the dying, unconcerned.

IV

Happy the soldier home, with not a notion
How somewhere, every dawn, some men attack,
And many sighs are drained.
Happy the lad whose mind was never trained :
His days are worth forgetting more than not.
He sings along the march
Which we march taciturn, because of dusk,
The long, forlorn, relentless trend
From larger day to huger night.

V

We wise, who with a thought besmirch
Blood over all our soul,
How should we see our task
But through his blunt and lashless eyes ?
Alive, he is not vital overmuch ;
Dying, not mortal overmuch ;

Nor sad, nor proud,
Nor curious at all.
He cannot tell
Old men's placidity from his.

VI

But cursed are dullards whom no cannon stuns,
That they should be as stones ;
Wretched are they, and mean
With paucity that never was simplicity.
By choice they made themselves immune
To pity and whatever moans in man
Before the last sea and the hapless stars ;
Whatever mourns when many leave these shores ;
Whatever shares
The eternal reciprocity of tears.

103. *Futility*

MOVE him into the sun—
Gently its touch awoke him once,
At home, whispering of fields unsown.
Always it woke him, even in France,
Until this morning and this snow.
If anything might rouse him now
The kind old sun will know.

Think how it wakes the seeds,—
Woke, once, the clays of a cold star.
Are limbs, so dear-achieved, are sides,
Full-nerved—still warm—too hard to stir ?

Was it for this the clay grew tall?
—O what made fatuous sunbeams toil
To break earth's sleep at all?

104. *Music*

I HAVE been urged by earnest violins
And drunk their mellow sorrows to the slake
Of all my sorrows and my thirsting sins.
My heart has beaten for a brave drum's sake.
Huge chords have wrought me mighty: I have hurled
Thuds of God's thunder. And with old winds pondered
Over the curse of this chaotic world,
With low lost winds that maundered as they wandered.

I have been gay with trivial fifes that laugh;
And songs more sweet than possible things are sweet;
And gongs, and oboes. Yet I guessed not half
Life's sympathy till I had made hearts beat,
And touched Love's body into trembling cries,
And blown my love's lips into laughs and sighs.

HERBERT E. PALMER

105. *Prayer for Rain*

O GOD, make it rain!
Loose the sott silver passion of the rain!
Send swiftly from above

This clear token of Thy love.
Make it rain!

Deck the bushes and the trees
With the tassels of the rain.
Make the brooks pound to the seas
And the earth shine young again.
God of passion, send the rain!

Oh, restore our ancient worth
With Thy rain!
Ease the heartache of the earth;
Sap the grain.
Fill the valleys and the dales
With Thy silver slanting gales;
And through England and wild Wales
Send the rain!

Lord, restore us to Thy will
With the rain!
Soak the valley, drench the hill,
Drown the stain;
Smite the mountain's withered hips,
Wash the rouge from sunset's lips,
Fill the sky with singing ships.
Send the rain!

106. *The Red Grouse*

I NEVER hear the red grouse yap upon a windy
moor
But a door goes clang in Elfinland, and I'm inside the
door,

I'm forty million miles away from all the wheels that run,
I'm one with winds and waterfalls, and swinging to the sun.

For the red grouse is a wilding bird that's mightier than the lark,
He's lightning to the weary heels, and drumfire in the dark ;
I dread no more the tarry wheels that grind the pine-ward track,
For the voice of God calls out of him, " Go back ! Go back ! Go back ! "

The moorland is the throne of God, where iron must fade away,
And there the red grouse challenges the tyrants of a day ;
The cars steal up the hazel dale, there's tar on every track,
But the moorland blows for bugle call, " Go back ! Go back ! Go back ! "

The voice of God did never warn or cry a thing in vain ;
He put the grouse on purple hills to make His meaning plain.
" Come not too near ! My reign is here, though Right be on the rack,
Beware ! Beware ! I'm width and air ! Go back ! Go back ! Go back ! "

107. *Through Curtains of Darkness*

(One for the Several)

THE voice of God came upon me through the darkness
That clothed the light of the lower air,
Stole upon me through corrupting darkness
As I walked prideful in despair,
Crying, " Take no heed of those who have stripped you,
Turn your back,—and see Me.
Though you be naked as the wind is naked
You shall be rainbow'd with the sea.

" Though men despise you, neglect you, frustrate you,
And remember you not in their books,
I have written your name on the granite hills
And the primrose banks of the brooks.
Therefore fear not, wail not, embitter not your just wrath,
Look in front and on high ;
For your songs are tangled in the lightning
And the cedar branches of the sky.

" To some has been given honour and riches,
Wealth of earth, strong sinew and power ;
But I have remembered my servant in the lean ditches
Even unto this blind hour.
Therefore rage not, chafe not, doubt not ;
You do wrong to feed your ire,
For I have given you an old song made new,
I have given you my heart's fire.

" Come unto Me all ye that labour,
Come unto Me and have rest.
Lay your head upon my starry tabor
And the celestial darkness of my breast.
Lean, rest, and be rocked upon Me
That the wind blow unto you of my ruth;
For I set my desire upon you
When you bit the bane of Truth.

" Truth is a poison unto the slack veins,
And a searing wildness to the soft eyes;
He that finds it shall be cut off,
And his breast torn with sighs.
For I see it not as the world sees it;
Men fear it and flee.
Come unto Me all ye that have seen it,
Come unto Me.

" Now are the days of darkness upon men,
There is no certainty in things done,
And the moon, a buckler of desolation,
Is a seduction unto the sun.
The stars fight in the lunar spaces;
The gnarled waves devour their sea.
Come unto Me all ye that are heavy laden,
Come unto Me.

" For he that finds Truth shall be shaken;
Demons shall stand at his ears;
Pride shall assail and cleave him;
He shall be thrust through with spears.
Therefore twist not, contort not, darken not

When you lift up your lyre;
For Truth was given unto the angels,
And they are melody and fire."

RUTH PITTER

108. *Sudden Heaven*

ALL was as it had ever been—
The worn familiar book,
The oak beyond the hawthorn seen,
The misty woodland's look:

The starling perched upon the tree
With his long tress of straw—
When suddenly heaven blazed on me,
And suddenly I saw:

Saw all as it would ever be,
In bliss too great to tell;
For ever safe, for ever free,
All bright with miracle:

Saw as in heaven the thorn arrayed,
The tree beside the door;
And I must die—but O my shade
Shall dwell there evermore.

109. *Early Rising*

I AROSE early, O my true love!
I was awake and wide

To see the last star quenched above
And the moon lying on her side.

I saw the tops of the tall elms shine
Over the mist on the lea,
And the new bells upon the bine
Opened most silently ;
And in the foggy dew the kine
Lay still as rocks in the sea.

The foggy dew lay on the flower
Silver and soft and chaste :
The turtle in her oaken tower
To waken made no haste :
Slept by her love another hour
And her two young embraced.

Mine was the solemn silence then,
And that clean tract of sky :
There was no smoke from hearths of men,
As yet no one went by :
The beast of night had sought his den,
The lark not climbed on high.

It was an hour of Eden ; yea,
So still the time and slow,
I thought the sun mistook his way,
And was bewildered so
That coming he might bring a day
Lost since a thousand years ago :

A day of innocence and mirth,
A birds' day, day of prayer,

When every simple tongue on earth
A song or psalm might bear :
When love of God was something worth,
And holiness not killed with care.

But even while musing so, I laid
Flame to the gathered wood :
The sullying smoke swept up the glade,
Abashed the morning stood :
And in the mead the milking-maid
Called up the kine with accents rude.

And I was sad, O my true love,
For the love left unsaid :
I will sing it to the turtle-dove
That hugs her high-built bed :
I will say it to the solemn grove
And to the innocent dead.

FREDERIC PROKOSCH

110. *The Dolls*

I FOUND them lying on the shore,
Sweet shapes, pearl-lipped and crescent-eyed :
Night after night their hands implore
Pathetic mercies at my side.

They reach into my secret night
With pale and terrifying arms
And offer in a dark delight
Their subtle suicidal charms,

Gently they sigh into my mind
Wild words half uttered, half unsaid,
And when I dream of death I find
Small tears of glass upon my bed.

They are the children of desire,
They live on fear, they are my deep
And buried thoughts with eyes of fire,
They are the furies of my sleep.

111. *The Watcher*

BLACK and still under the Siberian heaven
Lies the lake : rise the reeds : sleep the herons
(Wings aware of the coming flight past the high
Altai) ; and the sands still ; and not quite so still
The slopes cut by the icier streams where shadow
Covers the tread of the wolf, the quick nocturnal
Drinker ; in the shadow the streams descend through
the wood
Now lapped in the birch's arm, now sweet with cedar :

Sweet and cool the pools in the hill, and still
The sleeping dove beside the unloving deep.

I can see veins in the dark flesh of the world,
Warm and nervous, colour of dusk, violet.
I can hear the quick beat of the tremulous moment
As the land turns, as the night wheels on and hovers.
Through the weeds of China shine the strange yet
familiar

FREDERIC PROKOSCH

Lines of a face : the gaze, the trembling wet
Turn of the lips, the lids long parched with surrender
Which the years turn pale, which the night, the pale
night, covers.

I recall the sigh of the silently falling cities,
I can hear the deer, the delicate, at the well.

JOHN PUDNEY

112. *The Moonbathers*

THE spray, upon these moon-fired beaches, fills
The air like diamonds : and the bathers' sides,
Warmed by the genial ochre of the moon,
Splinter the frozen tides.

Here the quiet golden vegetation buds
And in the shade beneath the growing fronds
Of the convolvulus the bathers seek
Mirrors in the ice of ponds.

HERBERT READ

113. *The Seven Sleepers*

THE seven sleepers ere they left
the light and colour of the earth
the seven sleepers they did cry
(banishing their final fears) :

" Beauty will not ever fade.
To our cavern we retire
doomed to sleep ten thousand years.
Roll the rock across the gap

Then forget us ; we are quiet :
stiff and cold our bodies lie ;
Earth itself shall stir ere we
visit Earth's mortality.

Beauty when we wake will be
a solitude on land and sea."

114. *September Fires*

HAULMS burn
in distant fields.
Reluctantly the plumes of smoke
rise against a haze
of hills blue and clear
but featureless.

Our feet
crush the crinkled beech-leaves.
There is no other life than ours.
God is good to us this September evening
to give us a sun
and a world burning its dross.

Let us burn the twisted years
that have brought us to this meeting.

The crops are culled—
we can expect no other fruit
until another year
brings fire and fealty and the earth in barren stillness.

115. *The Falcon and the Dove*

I

THIS high-caught hooded Reason broods upon my wrist,
Fettered by a so tenuous leash of steel.
We are bound for the myrtle marshes, many leagues away,
And have a fair expectation of quarry.

II

Over the laggard dove, inclining to green boscage
Hovers this intentional doom—till the unsullied sky receives
A precipitation of shed feathers
And the swifter fall of wounded wings.

III

Will the plain aye echo with that loud *hullallo!*
Or retain an impress of our passage?
We have caught Beauty in a wild foray
And now the falcon is hooded and comforted away.

JAMES REEVES

116. *The Hour and the Storm*

SUMMER for England ends : simple and likeable
This moving a clock's hands, as if saying
" With this act we cancel formally the summer ;
We'll have no lingering last-rose last-post sweetness
Of breath-moist bugle flowering in the dusk.
Winterwards turn we the face of time."

The Hour bows over me,
Her eyes under the unfalling lashes
Are unreproachful and unbargaining :
She whom I always tried to elbow out
And cried against, this creature summons me
With how indifferent an imperiousness.
Useless to shield the face from that command.
Cry now, faint Human—nothing to cry unless
" Mercifully stifle with your fast embrace
This pitiful quivered protest or that shame,
Hour, blot out the tremulous mouth
That stills itself upon your heartlessness."

In the country early darkness brings the trees closer.
Walking homeward I feel them bending over me.
The fallen leaves startle my feet.
I hurry on for letters and late tea.
Soon the ground-mist covers the dying leaves.

The Storm protests the Hour :
But too wild a tattered breast to nestle in.
Only the wind supports ; that bitter staff
None falls with though he cry

" Fall, wind, that I may fall." His cries—
Anguish of unknown revelling, writhed rags of starved
    rebellion—
Tear from him, whirl with leaves, the flayed trees
Sob and shudder amidst the whelming rage.

O leaves, that the sun's fire fingered
And the loves of birds fêted, their music multiplied,
Wind-patterned endlessly against that blue
And sped along the idle stream
Where fish the frolic spun through fretted shallows :
Are you remembered of the sapless trees—
Their summer habit ? do you remember
Playing in the sun ? and playing was deceit ?

Hour, who are the Hour found again,
After the Storm's stolen interval,
Waiting, unblown, more merciless,
Will you forgive me if I say
" I am not less than trees divided
Between calm and wildness,
Smooth-falling leaves and heart like weather
Raging with the wind when comes
The Storm to voice hushed cries of fate."

MICHAEL ROBERTS

117. *Val d'Isère*

HERE is the world made real, not vision only :
    Here with the scented spruce and mountain-pink
And the rough touch of rock
The hills are one.

MICHAEL ROBERTS

From the far shining peak and burning rock-rib,
Here, in a patch of sunlight, in the pinewood,
The streams are glacier-cold,
And falling, talk.

Over the timeless blue, as through the mind,
Moves, in dissolving white, the summer cloud,
And the mind's eye is dark, and dazzled with
The simple truth :

Living at our full compass, we were one
With the four elements, and knew the rock,
And the sweet smell of earth,
And ice and fire ;

Graceful, blue Tsanteleina, beauty's pattern ;
Granta Parei, stark meditation ; and,
Dark as a falling breaker, fringed with foam,
Silent, snow-corniced Sassière.

Here, in the velvet dusk, the mingling bells
From the far grazing herd and the white chapel by the
    cataract will drown
In the last waves of sepia and violet and warm
Wild-honey gold.

Here, in the summer night, the spirit waits
The silence, and the beauty, and the moonlight,
Under Mont Pourri, and the wilderness of séracs, and
    the rock,
And cannot sleep.

118. *They Will Come Back*

THEY will come back, the quiet days,
Rosemary, myrtle, lavender,
And spring returning, leaf by leaf,
To the quiet heart, the single mind.

Not with the slow septennial change,
The steady pulse, or the iron tide ;
With the curfew dove, the quiet bell,
It will not come, the harvest-home.

They will not come, the gentian days,
With the cornfield white in summer, or the long
Provençal noon, but with the autumnal storm,
Strikes in the north, and random shots.

They will come back, the strenuous days,
On Peteret Ridge, the Eagle Nest,
And cross the gap of trivial time
Sure as the wind, the night express.

Through bombs, and teargas, through the acute
Machine-gun rattling answer, strict
Self-knowledge, dark rebellion, death
In the shuttered streets, through barricades,
And doors flung open in the wind,
They will come back.

119. *Hymn to the Sun*

"VOY wawm " said the dustman
one bright August morning—
But that was in Longbenton,
under the trees.

He was Northumbrian, he'd never known
horizons shimmering in the sun,
men with swart noontide faces sleeping, thick with
flies,
by roadside cherry trees.

He was Northumbrian, how should he know
mirage among blue hills,
thin streams that tinkle silence in the still
pulsating drone of summer—

How should he know
how cool the darkness in the white-washed inns
after the white road dancing, and the stones,
and quick dry lizards, round Millevaches ?

" *Fait chaud*," as each old woman said,
going over the hill, in Périgord,
prim in tight bonnets, worn black dresses, and content
with the lilt of sunlight in their bones.

120. *Victory*

DESOLATE are the fields of standing corn,
Lonely the twilit hills, and broken
The oaken lintel ;
Hushed are the harrying angels.

Silent, their vanguard halts :
There is no trap,
Lonely the placid stream and sorrowing hills,
Empty the thorp, the garth untended.

Desolate are the ways their spirit walks,
Desolate the road toward no city ;
For this they came ;
The lonely islands and deserted seas.

Defeat

IT was not thus we fought, nor in this city,
With the car-lines and the houses twisted,
And the entrails of the factory smouldering :
It was not here.

These bodies are not ours, lying, defeated,
Strangled by the unknown air, the drifting fumes,
These tortured lips and flowers are not us,
Our words were light.

These conquerors are not ours, nor these our children,
Building new barricades in stranger towns,
Our city dies in us, and in our eyes,
And dies defeated.

V. SACKVILLE-WEST

121. *From " The Land "*

THE country habit has me by the heart,
For he's bewitched forever who has seen,
Not with his eyes but with his vision, Spring

Flow down the woods and stipple leaves with
sun,
As each man knows the life that fits him best,
The shape it makes in his soul, the tune, the tone,
And after ranging on a tentative flight
Stoops like the merlin to the constant lure.
The country habit has me by the heart.
I never hear the sheep-bells in the fold,
Nor see the ungainly heron rise and flap
Over the marsh, nor hear the asprous corn
Clash, as the reapers set the sheaves in shocks
(That like a tented army dream away
The night beneath the moon in silvered fields),
Nor watch the stubborn team of horse and man
Graven upon the sky-line, nor regain
The sign-posts on the roads towards my home
Bearing familiar names—without a strong
Leaping of recognition ; only here
Lies peace after uneasy truancy ;
Here meet and marry many harmonies,
—All harmonies being ultimately one,—
Small mirroring majestic ; for as earth
Rolls on her journey, so her little fields
Ripen or sleep, and the necessities
Of seasons match the planetary law.
So truly stride between the earth and heaven
Sowers of grain : so truly in the spring
Earth's orbit swings both blood and sap to
rhythm,
And infinite and humble are at one ;
So the brown hedger, through the evening lanes
Homeward returning, sees above the ricks,
Sickle in hand, the sickle in the sky.

V. SACKVILLE-WEST

Shepherds and stars are quiet with the hills.
There is a bond between the men who go
From youth about the business of the earth,
And the earth they serve, their cradle and their grave;
Stars with the seasons alter; only he
Who wakeful follows the pricked revolving sky,
Turns concordant with the earth while others sleep;
To him the dawn is punctual; to him
The quarters of the year no empty name.
A loutish life, but in the midst of dark
Cut to a gash of beauty, as when the hawk
Bears upwards in its talons the striking snake,
High, and yet higher, till those two hang close,
Sculptural on the blue, together twined,
Exalted, deathly, silent, and alone.

And since to live men labour, only knowing
Life's little lantern between dark and dark,
The fieldsman in his grave humility
Goes about his centennial concerns,
Bread for his race and fodder for his kine,
Mating and breeding, since he only knows
The life he sees, how it may best endure,
(But on his Sabbath pacifies his God,
Blindly, though storm may wreck his urgent crops,)
And sees no beauty in his horny life,
With closer wisdom than soft poets use.
But I, like him, who strive
Closely with earth, and know her grudging mind,
Will sing no songs of bounty, for I see
Only the battle between man and earth,
The sweat, the weariness, the care, the balk;
See earth the slave and tyrant, mutinous,

Turning upon her tyrant and her slave,
Yielding reluctantly her fruits, to none
But most peremptory wooers.
Wherever waste eludes man's vigilance,
There spring the weeds and darnels ; where he treads
Through woods a tangle nets and trips his steps ;
His hands alone force fruitfulness and tilth ;
Strange lovers, man and earth ! their love and hate
Braided in mutual need ; and of their strife
A tired contentment born.

SIEGFRIED SASSOON

122. *The Power and the Glory*

L*ET there be life*, said God. And what He wrought
Went past in myriad marching lives, and brought
This hour, this quiet room, and my small thought
Holding invisible vastness in its hands.

Let there be God, say I. And what I've done
Goes onward like the splendour of the sun
And rises up in rapture and is one
With the white power of conscience that commands.

Let life be God. . . . What wail of fiend or wraith
Dare mock my glorious angel where he stands
To fill my dark with fire, my heart with faith ?

SIEGFRIED SASSOON

123. *The Merciful Knight*

SWIFT, in a moment's thought, our lastingness is wrought
From life, the transient wing.
Swift, in a moment's light, he mercy found, that knight
Who rode alone in spring . . .
The knight who sleeps in stone with ivy overgrown
Knew this miraculous thing.

In a moment of the years the sun, like love through tears,
Shone where the rain went by.
In a world where armoured men made swords their strength and then
Rode darkly out to die,
One heart was there estranged ; one heart, one heart was changed
While the cloud crossed the sun . . .
Mercy from long ago, be mine that I may know
Life's lastingness begun.

GEOFFREY SCOTT

124. *All our Joy is Enough*

ALL we make is enough
Barely to seem
A bee's din,
A beetle-scheme—

Sleepy stuff
For God to dream:
Begin.

All our joy is enough
At most to fill
A thimble cup
A little wind puff
Can shake, can spill:
Fill it up;
Be still.

All we know is enough;
Though written wide,
Small spider yet
With tangled stride
Will soon be off
The page's side:
Forget.

125. *Boats of Cane*

A TRAVELLER once told
How to an inland water slanting come
Slim boats of cane from rivers of Cathay,
With trembling mast so slight,
It seemed God made them with a hand of air
To sail upon His light;
And there
Soft they unload a jar of jade and gold
In the cold dawn when birds are dumb,
And then away,
And speak no word and seek no pay,

Away they steal
And leave no ripple at the keel.

So the tale is writ ;
And now, remembering you, I think of it.

EDITH SITWELL

126. *The Bat*

CASTELLATED, tall
From battlements fall
Shades on heroic
Lonely grass,
Where the moonlight's echoes die and pass.
Near the rustic boorish,
Fustian Moorish,
Castle wall of the ultimate Shade,
With his cloak castellated as that wall, afraid,
The mountebank doctor,
The old stage quack,
Where decoy duck dust
Began to clack,
Watched Heliogabalusene the Bat
In his furred cloak hang head down from the flat
Wall, cling to what is convenient,
Lenient.
" If you hang upside down with squeaking shrill,
You will see dust, lust, and the will to kill,
And life is a matter of which way falls
Your tufted turreted Shade near these walls.

For muttering guttering shadow will plan
If you're ruined wall, or pygmy man,"
Said Heliogabalusene, " or a pig,
Or the empty Cæsar in tall periwig."
And the mountebank doctor,
The old stage quack,
Spread out a black membraned wing of his cloak
And his shuffling footsteps seem to choke,
Near the Castle wall of the ultimate Shade
Where decoy duck dust
Quacks, clacks, afraid.

127. *The King of China's Daughter*

THE King of China's daughter,
She never would love me
Though I hung my cap and bells upon
Her nutmeg tree.
For oranges and lemons,
The stars in bright blue air,
(I stole them long ago, my dear)
Were dangling there.
The moon did give me silver pence,
The sun did give me gold,
And both together softly blew
And made my porridge cold ;
But the King of China's daughter
Pretended not to see
When I hung my cap and bells upon
Her nutmeg tree.

128. *The Little Ghost who Died for Love*

[Deborah Churchill, born in 1678, was hanged in 1708 for shielding her lover in a duel. His opponent was killed, her lover fled to Holland, and she was hanged in his stead, according to the law of the time. The chronicle said, " Though she died at peace with God, this malefactor could never understand the justice of her sentence, to the last moment of her life."]

" FEAR not, O maidens, shivering
As bunches of the dew-drenched leaves
In the calm moonlight . . . it is the cold sends quivering
My voice, a little nightingale that grieves.

Now Time beats not, and dead Love is forgotten . . .
The spirit too is dead and dank and rotten,

And I forget the moment when I ran
Between my lover and the sworded man—
Blinded with terror lest I lose his heart.
The sworded man dropped, and I saw depart

Love and my lover and my life . . . he fled
And I was strung and hung upon the tree.
It is so cold now that my heart is dead
And drops through time . . . night is too dark to see

Him still. . . . But it is spring ; upon the fruit-boughs
of your lips,
Young maids, the dew like India's splendour drips ;
Pass by among the strawberry beds, and pluck the
berries
Cooled by the silver moon ; pluck boughs of cherries

That seem the lovely lucent coral bough
(From streams of starry milk those branches grow)
That Cassiopeia feeds with her faint light,
Like Ethiopia ever jewelled bright.

Those lovely cherries do enclose
Deep in their sweet hearts the silver snows,

And the small budding flowers upon the trees
Are filled with sweetness like the bags of bees.

Forget my fate . . . but I, a moonlight ghost,
Creep down the strawberry paths and seek the lost

World, the apothecary at the Fair.
I, Deborah, in my long cloak of brown
Like the small nightingale that dances down
The cherried boughs, creep to the doctor's bare
Booth . . . cold as ivy in the air,

And, where I stand, the brown and ragged light
Holds something still beyond, hid from my sight.

Once, plumaged like the sea, his swanskin head
Had wintry white quills . . . 'Hearken to the
Dead . . .
I was a nightingale, but now I croak
Like some dark harpy hidden in night's cloak,
Upon the walls ; among the Dead, am quick ;
Oh, give me medicine, for the world is sick ;
Not medicines, planet-spotted like fritillaries
For country sins and old stupidities,
Nor potions you may give a country maid

When she is love-sick . . . love in earth is laid,
Grown dead and rotten' . . . so I sank me down,
Poor Deborah in my long cloak of brown.
Though cockcrow marches, crying of false dawns,
Shall bury my dark voice, yet still it mourns
Among the ruins,—for it is not I
But this old world, is sick and soon must die ! "

129. *From "The Sleeping Beauty"*

IN the great gardens, after bright spring rain,
We find sweet innocence come once again,
White periwinkles, little pensionnaires
With muslin gowns and shy and candid airs,

That under saint-blue skies, with gold stars sown,
Hide their sweet innocence by spring winds blown,
From zephyr libertines that like Richelieu
And d'Orsay their gold-spangled kisses blew ;

And lilies of the valley whose buds blonde and tight
Seem curls of little school-children that light
The priests' procession, when on some saint's day
Along the country paths they make their way ;

Forget-me-nots, whose eyes of childish blue,
Gold-starred like heaven, speak of love still true ;
And all the flowers that we call " dear heart,"
Who say their prayers like children, then depart

Into the dark. Amid the dew's bright beams
The summer airs, like Weber waltzes, fall

Round the first rose who flushed with her youth seems
Like young Princesses dressed for their first ball :

Who knows what beauty ripens from dark mould
After the sad wind and the winter's cold ?—
But a small wind sighed, colder than the rose
Blooming in desolation, " No one knows."

OSBERT SITWELL

130. *Mary-Anne*

I

MARY-ANNE,
Wise, simple old woman,
Lived in a patchwork pavilion,
Pitched on an island,
Feeding the piebald and the tartan ducks.

Flotillas of ducks
Lie low in the water,
And Mary-Anne seems
The Duck-King's daughter.
The floating ducks crack up in their arrow-pointed
wake
The distorted, silent summer painted in the lake,
And the days disappear
In a leaden stare.

Then Mary-Anne waddles
Through the evening cool,
And a smell of musk

Lingers by the pool,
For the trembling fingers of the honeysuckle
Wring out the blue and the dew-drenched dusk.

At night the pavilion
Is hung by a silver cord
That the nightingales plait
With their intercoiling song.
Within Mary-Anne mutters
The Word of the Lord,
Till the candle gutters,
As the summer sighs outside
And taps
At the shutters.

II

The silver-threaded wire
With which the nightingales
Suspended her pavilion
Was not the sole support it seemed:
For there was a direct attachment,
An umbilical cord to Heaven.
Her webfooted world
Teemed with four-leafed clovers,
With tea-leaves, cards, new moons,
And every sort of augury.
For was she not
The Seventh Child of a Seventh Child
Born under Venus,
Had she not seen the Blue Man ride
Away, the bleak night that the late lord died?
Not frightened, never in the least,

But seeing things,
Constantly.

Opposite on the shore
Was the Cedar Avenue,
Where fallen fragrance hushed the footsteps,
And there,
Quite often of an evening,
Mary-Anne could see
The Cavalier lord walking,
More conventional in death than in life ever,
Carrying his handsome head beneath an out-turned arm.
It was he who had done all this for Mary-Anne,
    Who had made the lake and given it countless
        things to mirror ;
    Who had made the broken flights of steps,
    The balustrades, the floating-terraces
    And colonnades, wherein Italian winds
    Whispered and sang their arias—
    Winds that he had netted centuries ago
    In the plumed grottoes of a Roman garden—
    And statues that the years had fretted
    To limbless, eyeless, lipless lepers.
It was he, too, who had planted the park with hawthorns
That prance like red and white chessmen
Through the chequered springtime.

III

In the winter her pavilion
Was a tent of swansdown.
The windows tightly closed
Showed through their brittle yellow ice

A fern, and cubèd walls.
The wild geese thrust their long necks
Out into the cold air above,
And the white feathers drifted up to the window.
Then the Family would come down,
Like so many cats after the birds, she always said.
The snowflakes would sway down
And thud,
            thud,
                    thud
                          would sound the falling pheasants.

131. *Mrs. Southern's Enemy*

EVEN as the shadows of the statues lengthen,
While, when the glowing glass below is broken,
The plunging images are shaken,
For the young, blue-wingèd god is woken,
Sighs, stretches, shivers, till his muscles strengthen
So he can trample down the flowers, forsaken
By their droning, golden-liveried lovers, tumble
Among them till their red mouths tremble,
Already in the ancient house, whose shadow dies
With the slow opening of its hundred eyes,
Already, even then, Night the Black Panther
Is slinking, creeping down the corridors,
Lithe-swinging on her velvet paws,
Sharpening her treacherous claws
To frighten children.

And then it is
                    I seem to see again
That grey typhoon we knew as Mrs. Southern,

Spinning along the darkened passages,
Watching things, tugging things,
Seeing to things,
                    And putting things to rights.

Oh, would that the cruel daylight, too,
Could give us back again
Dear Mrs. Southern,
Dear selfless, blue-lipped Mrs. Southern,
Cross, mumbling and transparent Mrs. Southern,
With her grey hair,
                    Grey face,
                              And thinly-bitter smile,
In wide blue skirt, white-spotted, and white apron ;
On the very top of her head she carried a cap,
An emblem of respect and respectability, while
As though she were a Hindu charmer of snakes,
Her hair lay coiled and tame at the back of her head.
But her actual majesty was really the golden glory,
Through which she moved, a hurrying fly
Enshrined in rolling amber,
As she spun along in a twisting column of golden
    atoms,
A halo of gold motes above and about her,
A column of visible, virtuous activity.
Her life was a span of hopeless conflict,
For she battled against Time,
That never-vanquished and invisible foe,
She did not recognise her enemy,
She thought him Dust :
But what is Dust,
Save Time's most lethal weapon,
His faithful ally and our sneaking foe,

Through whom Time steals and covers all we know,
The very instrument through whom he overcame
Great Nineveh and Rome and Carthage,
Ophir and Trebizond and Ephesus,
Now deep, all deep, so deep in dust?
    Even the lean and arid archæologist,
    Who bends above the stones, and peers and
        ponders,
    Will be his, too, one day.
Dust loads the dice,
Then challenges to play,
Each layer of dust upon a chair or table
A tablet to his future victory.
And Dust is cruel, no victory despising,
However slight,
And Dust is greedy, eats the very bones;
So that, in the end, still not content
With trophies such as Helen of Troy,
Or with the conquering golden flesh of Cleopatra
    (She, perhaps, understood the age-long battle,
    For did she not prefer to watch her pearl
    Dissolve in amber wine,
    Thus herself enjoying
    Its ultimate disintegration,
    Than let Dust conquer such a thing of beauty?
    Was not the asp, fruit-hidden,
    The symbol of such understanding?),
He needs must seize on Mrs. Southern,
Poor mumbling, struggling, blue-lipped Mrs.
    Southern,
For Dust is insatiate and invincible.

132. *Beethoven's Death Mask*

I IMAGINE him still with heavy brow.
Huge, black, with bent head and falling hair
He ploughs the landscape. His face
Is this hanging mask transfigured,
This mask of death which the white lights make stare.

I see the thick hands clasped ; the scare-crow coat ;
The light strike upwards at the holes for eyes ;
The beast squat in that mouth, whose opening is
The hollow opening of an organ pipe :
There the wind sings and the harsh longing cries.

He moves across my vision like a ship.
What else is iron but he ? The fields divide
And, heaving, are changing waters of the sea.
He is prisoned, masked, shut off from being ;
Life like a fountain he sees leap—outside.

Yet, in that head there twists the roaring cloud
And coils, as in a shell, the roaring wave.
The damp leaves whisper ; bending to the rain
The April rises in him, chokes his lungs
And climbs the torturing passage of his brain.

Then the drums move away, the Distance shows ;
Now cloudy peaks are bared ; the mystic One
Horizons haze, as the blue incense heaven.
Peace, peace . . . Then splitting skull and dream, there
comes,
Blotting our lights, the trumpeter, the sun.

133. *I Think Continually*

I THINK continually of those who were truly great.
Who, from the womb, remembered the soul's history
Through corridors of light where the hours are suns
Endless and singing. Whose lovely ambition
Was that their lips, still touched with fire,
Should tell of the Spirit clothed from head to foot in song.
And who hoarded from the Spring branches
The desires falling across their bodies like blossoms.

What is precious is never to forget
The essential delight of the blood drawn from ageless springs
Breaking through rocks in worlds before our earth.
Never to deny its pleasure in the morning simple light
Nor its grave evening demand for love.
Never to allow gradually the traffic to smother
With noise and fog the flowering of the spirit.

Near the snow, near the sun, in the highest fields
See how these names are fêted by the waving grass
And by the streamers of white cloud
And whispers of wind in the listening sky.
The names of those who in their lives fought for life
Who wore at their hearts the fire's centre.
Born of the sun they travelled a short while towards the sun,
And left the vivid air signed with their honour.

134. *My Parents*

MY parents kept me from children who were rough
And who threw words like stones and who wore torn clothes.
Their thighs showed through rags. They ran in the street
And climbed cliffs and stripped by the country streams.

I feared more than tigers their muscles like iron
And their jerking hands and their knees tight on my arms.
I feared the salt coarse pointing of those boys
Who copied my lisp behind me on the road.

They were lithe, they sprang out behind hedges
Like dogs to bark at our world. They threw mud
And I looked another way, pretending to smile.
I longed to forgive them, yet they never smiled.

135. *The Express*

AFTER the first powerful plain manifesto
The black statement of pistons, without more fuss
But gliding like a queen, she leaves the station.
Without bowing and with restrained unconcern
She passes the houses which humbly crowd outside,
The gasworks and at last the heavy page
Of death, printed by gravestones in the cemetery.
Beyond the town there lies the open country
Where, gathering speed, she acquires mystery,
The luminous self-possession of ships on ocean.

It is now she begins to sing—at first quite low
Then loud, and at last with a jazzy madness—
The song of her whistle screaming at curves,
Of deafening tunnels, brakes, innumerable bolts.
And always light, aerial, underneath
Goes the elate metre of her wheels.
Steaming through metal landscape on her lines
She plunges new eras of wild happiness
Where speed throws up strange shapes, broad curves
And parallels clean like the steel of guns.
At last, further than Edinburgh or Rome,
Beyond the crest of the world, she reaches night
Where only a low streamline brightness
Of phosphorus on the tossing hills is white.
Ah, like a comet through flame, she moves entranced
Wrapt in her music no bird song, no, nor bough
Breaking with honey buds, shall ever equal.

136. *The Pylons*

THE secret of these hills was stone, and cottages
Of that stone made,
And crumbling roads
That turned on sudden hidden villages.

Now over these small hills they have built the concrete
That trails black wire :
Pylons, those pillars
Bare like nude, giant girls that have no secret.

The valley with its gilt and evening look
And the green chestnut

Of customary root
Are mocked dry like the parched bed of a brook.

But far above and far as sight endures
Like whips of anger
With lightning's danger
There runs the quick perspective of the future.

This dwarfs our emerald country by its trek
So tall with prophecy :
Dreaming of cities
Where often clouds shall lean their swan-white neck.

L. A. G. STRONG

137. *The Mad-Woman*

A SWELL within her billowed skirts
  Like a great ship with sails unfurled,
The mad-woman goes gallantly
  Upon the ridges of her world.

With eagle nose and wisps of gray
  She strides upon the westward hills,
Swings her umbrella joyously
  And waves it to the waving mills,

Talking and chuckling as she goes
  Indifferent both to sun and rain,
With all that merry company
  The singing children of her brain.

138. *The Blunder*

SOME god, quite irresponsible and young,
Has jumbled time and place and dealt amiss :
A day of Grecian spring-time he has flung
Into this winter-bound Metropolis.
O blessèd blunderer ! To-day the air
Is blue as the Aegean, soft as wine,
And there are Tritons in Trafalgar Square
And white-limbed Naiads in the Serpentine.
To-day great Centaurs gallop down the Row ;
Hyde Park's a silver mist of olive-trees ;
And all the costers' barrows overflow
With golden apples from the Hesperides.
Hide, careless god ! There'll be, without a doubt,
Hades to pay in heaven when Zeus finds out !

139. *London Lovers*

COUNTRY lovers play at love
In a scene all laid for loving.
Marriage-making stars above
Gossip and wink and look approving,
While the moon with maudlin beam
Gilds the sentimental air,
And lends the glamour of a dream
To eye and hand, to lip and hair ;
Long dewy lanes invite the feet
And all the silver dusk is sweet
With unimaginable roses ;

And round the heart enchantment closes,
And the whole world's a lovers' tale
Spun by the moon and the nightingale.

O love's a simple word to say
With nature aiding and abetting ;
And love's an easy part to play
On such a stage, in such a setting.

London lovers lack the aid
Of such poetic properties :
In uninspiring streets are played
Their love-scenes and their ecstasies.
They are not coached by moon or star
Or prompted by the nightingale ;
On Shepherd's Bush no roses are ;
There lies no dew in Maida Vale.
London lovers see instead
Electric sky-signs overhead,
Jarring upon romantic mood
With eulogies of patent food.
For them no peace when twilight falls,
Only the noise of busy places,
The drabness of a thousand walls,
The staring of a thousand faces.
Yet London man to London maid
Makes his undaunted serenade :
Enraptured and oblivious
He woos her—on a motor-bus.

O proudly down each thoroughfare
Go London lovers two by two :
For London love is staunch and rare

And brave and difficult and true;
And seven times sweet is each caress
Snatched from a world of ugliness.

DOROTHY MARGARET STUART

140. *Nine Men's Morrice*

(1655)

OUR maypole with much labour
Is now in faggots hewn;
No more to pipe and tabor,
With bells upon their shoon,
The lads dance round on Mayday, and wag green boughs on Mayday,
To Sellinger his tune.

They may not leap or wrestle;
No quintain swings to-day;
No mummer sets a trestle
Upon the green to play;
But we play nine men's morrice, we *will* play nine men's morrice,
Though NOLL himself say Nay.

The turf is smoothly shaven
As it was wont to be;
The squares are trimly graven;
The stones are three times three;
And there we elders set them and take them up and set them,
Each kneeling on his knee.

DOROTHY MARGARET STUART

The youngsters go to sermon
For lack of better sport,
But we old men determine
That, since our time be short,
We'll have our good old pastime—it was a courtly pastime
When England *had* a Court.

We have no pretty posies
Against our belts of buff,
Upon our shoes no roses,
No lace on coat or cuff;
But we three old companions will play *like* old companions,
Let NOLL speak ne'er so gruff.

Some Puritan new-shavèd
May o'er the box-hedge peep;
Then with a psalm of DAVID
We sing his doubts to sleep,
And gravely move our pieces, and lift and shift our pieces,
All chanting loud and deep.

And, if that whey-faced brother
Stand glooming for a spell,
We talk to one another
O' the Kings of Israel,
Or rail at Squire and Parson, and swear that Squire and Parson
Were worshippers of Bel.

DOROTHY MARGARET STUART

Now Heaven grant, good neighbours,
   That maypoles rise again,
That fiddles, pipes and tabors
   Take up their old refrain,
And that KING CHARLES win homeward, ah! when
      KING CHARLES wins homeward
   The fiddlers will be fain.

A. S. J. TESSIMOND

141. *Cats no less Liquid than their Shadows*

CATS, no less liquid than their shadows,
   Offer no angles to the wind.
They slip, diminished, neat, through loopholes
   Less than themselves ; will not be pinned

To rules or routes for journeys ; counter
   Attack with non-resistance ; twist
Enticing through the curving fingers
   And leave an angered, empty fist.

They wait, obsequious as darkness,
   Quick to retire, quick to return ;
Admit no aim or ethics ; flatter
   With reservations ; will not learn

To answer to their names ; are seldom
   Truly owned till shot and skinned.
Cats, no less liquid than their shadows,
   Offer no angles to the wind.

A. S. J. TESSIMOND

142. *Epitaph on a Disturber of his Times*

WE expected the violin's finger on the upturned nerve;
Its importunate cry, too laxly curved:
And you drew us an oboe-outline, clean and acute;
Unadorned statement, accurately carved.

We expected the screen, the background for reverie
Which cloudforms usefully weave:
And you built the immaculate, adamant, blue-green steel
Arch of a balanced wave.

We expected a pool with flowers to diffuse and break
The child-round face of the mirrored moon:
And you blazed a rock-path, begun near the sun, to be finished
By the trained and intrepid feet of men.

DYLAN THOMAS

143. *Poem in October*

ESPECIALLY when the October wind
With frosty fingers punishes my hair,
Caught by the crabbing sun I walk on fire
And cast a shadow crab upon the land,
By the sea's side, hearing the noise of birds,
Hearing the raven cough in winter sticks,
My busy heart who shudders as she talks
Sheds the syllabic blood and drains her words.

Shut, too, in a tower of words, I mark
On the horizon walking like the trees
The wordy shapes of women, and the rows
Of the star-gestured children in the park.
Some let me make you of the vowelled beeches,
Some of the oaken voices, from the roots
Of many a thorny shire tell you notes,
Some let me make you of the water's speeches.

Behind a pot of ferns the wagging clock
Tells me the hour's word, the neural meaning
Flies on the shafted disc, declaims the morning
And tells the windy weather in the cock.
Some let me make you of the meadow's signs ;
The signal grass that tells me all I know
Breaks with the wormy winter through the eye.
Some let me spell you of the raven's sins.

Especially when the October wind
(Some let me make you of autumnal vowels,
The spider-tongued, and the loud hill of Wales)
With fist of turnips punishes the land,
Some let me make you of the heartless words.
The heart is drained that, spelling in the scurry
Of chemic blood, warned of the coming fury.
By the sea's side hear the dark-vowelled birds.

144. *We Lying by Seasand*

WE lying by seasand, watching yellow
And the grave sea, mock who deride
Who follow the red rivers, hollow
Alcove of words out of cicada shade,

For in this yellow grave of sand and sea
A calling for colour calls with the wind
That's grave and gay as grave and sea
Sleeping on either hand.
The lunar silences, the silent tide
Lapping the still canals, the dry tide-master
Ribbed between desert and water storm,
Should cure our ills of the water
With a one-coloured calm ;
The heavenly music over the sand
Sounds with the grains as they hurry
Hiding the golden mountains and mansions
Of the grave, gay seaside land.
Bound by a sovereign strip, we lie,
Watch yellow, wish for wind to blow away
The strata of the shore and leave red rock ;
But wishes breed not, neither
Can we fend off the rock arrival,
Lie watching yellow until the golden weather
Breaks, O my heart's blood, like a heart and hill.

W. J. TURNER

145. *Nostalgia*

AS one goes on
It becomes increasingly dark,
The summers are darker-leafed,
The springs rain-clouded,
The days and nights lie closer together,
The years are swept away like husks.

W. J. TURNER

It is raining everywhere.

When the sun shines it is like a ghost returning,
Everywhere there are umbrellas ;
Nobody heeds that pale recollection
Gliding over their heads.

In the days of my youth it came as an enchanter,
Everybody threw their hats into the sky,
The flowers burst into colour
The hills rose billowing in green pavilions
The streams ran glittering crystal
The birds carolled gambolling in the air !

I pull my hat over my eyes
The rain is come for ever
For ever and ever.

•

JAMES WALKER

146. *World without End*

BEYOND these walls I feel
The serpent night uncurl
Its myriad coils of darkness as it crawls
Close, close, on twilight's heel ;
I hear beyond these walls
Wind like a demon wail,
Wind like a great bat hurl
Against the stone and fail
To find a lodging there ;

JAMES WALKER

Beyond these walls I know
For mile on jagged mile
The ling-scarred mountains roll
Wild, dark, inarable.

And out within their folds
The Wrath undreamed-of preys
That has bided and lain low
Through aeons of nights and days :
Each rumbling blast that shook
The crystal sky is known,
For every leaf-light shock
Of human foot set down
Upon this pristine rock
Late, soon, man must atone—
For earth at last shall tire
Of man, her darling guest,
And time spin back this star
To chaos with the rest.

REX WARNER

147. *Chough*

DESOLATE that cry as though world were unworthy.
See now, rounding the headland, a forlorn hopeless bird,
trembling black wings fingering the blowy air,
dainty and ghostly, careless of the scattering salt.

This is the cave-dweller that flies like a butterfly,
buffeted by daws, almost extinct, who has chosen,
so gentle a bird, to live on furious coasts.

Here where sea whistles in funnels, and slaps the back
of burly granite slabs, and hisses over holes,
in bellowing hollows that shelter the female seal
the Cornish chough wavers over the waves.

By lion rocks, rocks like the heads of queens,
sailing with ragged plumes upturned, into the wind
goes delicate indifferent the doomed bird.

148. *Dipper*

URBANE, rotund, secretive, dashing dipper,
O daintier and gentler than the aldermen
we know in our life, bowing not to a Highness
but to wealth of running water in shine or shower,
the gliding race shaken into shiver of foam below your
feet.

Dapper you go, stout, bowing at the edge of cascades,
neat, melancholy bird.

Sometimes in unruffled water, scrabbling with your toes
for gravel, down you dive, and stride along the bottom,
keeping the land's conventions even in liquid.

Low-flying, even in air to earth and water true,
you dash through mossy grooves, olive tunnels of shade,
shy haunter of broken water, faithful to home
where screened by snowy smoke of falls in nook you
nest.

REX WARNER

149. *Mallard*

SQUAWKING they rise from reeds into the sun,
climbing like furies, running on blood and bone,
with wings like garden shears clipping the misty air,
four mallard, hard winged, with necks like rods
fly in perfect formation over the marsh.

Keeping their distance, gyring, not letting slip the air,
but leaping into it straight like hounds or divers,
they stretch out into the wind and sound their horns
again.

Suddenly siding to a bank of air unbidden
by hand signal or morse message of command
downsky they plane, sliding like corks on a current,
designed so deftly that all air is advantage,

till, with few flaps, orderly as they left earth,
alighting among curlew they pad on mud.

DOROTHY WELLESLEY

150. *Lenin*

(February 1927)

IT was night when I saw Lenin,
The Red Square dark but for snow.
Kremlin walls invisible, only the tower
Merged to light at the top. There, light flung upward

DOROTHY WELLESLEY

From a lantern unseen threw its glow
On a flag, which flew on the sky,
As colours turn in the dark,
A curious unnatural scarlet.

I went through the door to Lenin.
Each side of the door
Were stationed, like figures from Noah's Ark,
Two sentries, their skirts hooping out
To a mass of solidity round their feet for the cold:
Wooden toys set firm on the base.
And I smiled as I passed through the door.

So I came down the steps to Lenin.
With a herd of peasants before
And behind me, I saw
A room stained scarlet, and there
A small wax man in a small glass case.
Two sentinels at his feet, and one at his head,
Two little hands on his breast:
Pious spinster asleep; and I said
" Many warrants these delicate hands have signed."
A lamp shone, red,
An aureole over him, on his red hair;
His uniform clothed him still.

Greedy of detail I saw,
In those two minutes allowed,
The man was not wax, as they said,
But a corpse, for a thumb nail was black,
The thing was Lenin.

Then a woman beside me cried
With a strange voice, foreign, loud.

And I, who fear not life nor death, and those who have died
Only a little, was inwardly shaken with fear,
For I stood in the presence of God;
The voice I heard was the voice of all generations
Acclaiming new faiths, horrible, beautiful faiths;
I knew that the woman wailed as women wailed long ago
For Christ in the sepulchre laid.
Christ was a wax man too,
When they carried Him down to the grave.

Christ came not to save,
Christ was terrible too,
He brought not peace but a sword.

Then I knew that I too should wail with the peasant women,
Not for Lenin, not for our Lord,
But wail in my heart for the fireside personal gods:
For Apollo, who leaned on the lintels of farms, in the evening light,
Begging a flagon of wine. Or, for her,
Aphrodite Anadyomene,
White in her shell.

Where goeth man? This I know:
It was night when I saw Lenin,
The Red Square dark but for snow.

LAURENCE WHISTLER

151. *The Glass Chandelier*

THE fire upon the books
Lifts its hurried looks :
It reads by tiny flames
The sad and golden names.
The wind at the window bars
Troubles the glass of stars.
The stars in the window pane
Alter like rain.

Fire, wind and star
Much in movement are.
Flesh of man the same—
Flash as star and flame
And faring like the wind
Now crowned with stars, now blind.
But wind cannot force,
Nor star to any course,
Though fire all night must show
The glass chandelier—
Like a larch in snow,
And a saint in air,
Or a very still lady.
A kind of beauty
Too near the look of death,
Too still, for us whose breath
Is troubled with desire
And brief as wind and fire.

152. *The Painted Flower*

NOT the flower itself but the thought
of your flower that I have made
I have brought.
In their brief masquerade
men and the heather
put on the dominoes
of flesh and the blade's green feather.
And those
before the owl has cried
are laid aside.

But here, time overthrown,
green flame and bloom's white spark
disown
the slow atomic dark.
Division and the grief
of dust will not prevail
on bud or leaf
nor overset the pale
but mandatory power
of an imagined flower.

The Indian conjurer
makes a bush with two passes
grow quicklier
than under sun the jungle grasses—
in momentary magic. This
is not such : having no mortal part
nor weaknesses.

And the old fowler of the heart
can use a blossom as lime
to snare the wings of time.

W. B. YEATS

153. *Byzantium*

THE unpurged images of day recede;
The Emperor's drunken soldiery are abed;
Night resonance recedes, night-walkers' song
After great cathedral gong;
A starlit or a moonlit dome disdains
All that man is,
All mere complexities,
The fury and the mire of human veins.

Before me floats an image, man or shade,
Shade more than man, more image than a shade;
For Hades' bobbin bound in mummy-cloth
May unwind the winding path;
A mouth that has no moisture and no breath
Breathless mouths may summon;
I hail the superhuman;
I call it death-in-life and life-in-death.

Miracle, bird or golden handiwork,
More miracle than bird or handiwork,
Planted on the star-lit golden bough,
Can like the cocks of Hades crow,
Or, by the moon embittered, scorn aloud

In glory of changeless metal
Common bird or petal
And all complexities of mire or blood.

At midnight on the Emperor's pavement flit
Flames that no faggot feeds, nor steel has lit,
Nor storm disturbs, flames begotten of flame,
Where blood-begotten spirits come
And all complexities of fury leave,
Dying into a dance,
An agony of trance,
An agony of flame that cannot singe a sleeve.

Astraddle on the dolphin's mire and blood,
Spirit after spirit! The smithies break the flood,
The golden smithies of the Emperor!
Marbles of the dancing floor
Break bitter furies of complexity,
Those images that yet
Fresh images beget,
That dolphin-torn, that gong-tormented sea.

154. *Coole and Ballylee, 1931*

UNDER my window-ledge the waters race,
Otters below and moor-hens on the top,
Run for a mile undimmed in Heaven's face
Then darkening through 'dark' Raftery's 'cellar' drop,
Run underground, rise in a rocky place
In Coole demesne, and there to finish up

Spread to a lake and drop into a hole.
What's water but the generated soul?

Upon the border of that lake's a wood
Now all dry sticks under a wintry sun,
And in a copse of beeches there I stood,
For Nature's pulled her tragic buskin on
And all the rant's a mirror of my mood:
At sudden thunder of the mounting swan
I turned about and looked where branches break
The glittering reaches of the flooded lake.

Another emblem there! That stormy white
But seems a concentration of the sky;
And, like the soul, it sails into the sight
And in the morning's gone, no man knows why;
And is so lovely that it sets to right
What knowledge or its lack had set awry,
So arrogantly pure, a child might think
It can be murdered with a spot of ink.

Sound of a stick upon the floor, a sound
From somebody that toils from chair to chair;
Beloved books that famous hands have bound,
Old marble heads, old pictures everywhere;
Great rooms where travelled men and children found
Content or joy; a last inheritor
Where none has reigned that lacked a name and fame
Or out of folly into folly came.

A spot whereon the founders lived and died
Seemed once more dear than life; ancestral trees,
Or gardens rich in memory glorified

Marriages, alliances and families,
And every bride's ambition satisfied.
Where fashion or mere fantasy decrees
Man shifts about—all that great glory spent—
Like some poor Arab tribesman and his tent.

We were the last romantics—chose for theme
Traditional sanctity and loveliness ;
Whatever's written in what poets name
The book of the people ; whatever most can bless
The mind of man or elevate a rhyme ;
But all is changed, that high horse riderless,
Though mounted in that saddle Homer rode
Where the swan drifts upon a darkening flood.

155. *For Anne Gregory*

"NEVER shall a young man,
Thrown into despair
By those great honey-coloured
Ramparts at your ear,
Love you for yourself alone
And not your yellow hair."

" But I can get a hair-dye
And set such colour there,
Brown, or black, or carrot,
That young men in despair
May love me for myself alone
And not my yellow hair."

" I heard an old religious man
But yesternight declare

That he had found a text to prove
That only God, my dear,
Could love you for yourself alone
And not your yellow hair."

156. *A Prayer for Old Age*

GOD guard me from those thoughts men think
In the mind alone;
He that sings a lasting song
Thinks in a marrow-bone;

From all that makes a wise old man
That can be praised of all;
O what am I that I should not seem
For the song's sake a fool?

I pray—for fashion's word is out
And prayer comes round again—
That I may seem, though I die old,
A foolish, passionate man.

157. *Sailing to Byzantium*

I

THAT is no country for old men. The young
In one another's arms, birds in the trees,
—Those dying generations—at their song,
The salmon-falls, the mackerel-crowded seas,
Fish, flesh, or fowl, commend all summer long

Whatever is begotten, born, and dies.
Caught in that sensual music all neglect
Monuments of unageing intellect.

II

An aged man is but a paltry thing,
A tattered coat upon a stick, unless
Soul clap its hands and sing, and louder sing
For every tatter in its mortal dress,
Nor is there singing school but studying
Monuments of its own magnificence ;
And therefore I have sailed the seas and come
To the holy city of Byzantium.

III

O sages standing in God's holy fire
As in the gold mosaic of a wall,
Come from the holy fire, perne in a gyre,
And be the singing-masters of my soul.
Consume my heart away ; sick with desire
And fastened to a dying animal
It knows not what it is ; and gather me
Into the artifice of eternity.

IV

Once out of nature I shall never take
My bodily form from any natural thing,
But such a form as Grecian goldsmiths make
Of hammered gold and gold enamelling
To keep a drowsy Emperor awake ;
Or set upon a golden bough to sing
To lords and ladies of Byzantium
Of what is past, or passing, or to come.

W. B. YEATS

158. *Song from "A Full Moon in March"*

O, BUT I saw a solemn sight;
Said the rambling, shambling travelling-man;
Castle Dargan's ruin all lit,
Lovely ladies dancing in it.

What though they danced! Those days are gone,
Said the wicked, crooked, hawthorn tree;
Lovely lady or gallant man
Are blown cold dust or a bit of bone.

O, what is life but a mouthful of air?
Said the rambling, shambling travelling-man;
Yet all the lovely things that were
Live, for I saw them dancing there.

Nobody knows what may befall,
Said the wicked, crooked, hawthorn tree.
I have stood so long by a gap in the wall
Maybe I shall not die at all.

ANDREW YOUNG

159. *Late Autumn*

THE boy called to his team
  And with blue-glancing share
Turned up the rape and turnip
  With yellow charlock to spare.

The long lean thistles stood
   Like beggars ragged and blind,
Half their white silken locks
   Blown away on the wind.

But I thought not once of winter
   Or summer that was past
Till I saw that slant-legged robin
   With autumn on his chest.

160. *The Stockdoves*

THEY rose up in a twinkling cloud
   And wheeled about and bowed
To settle on the trees
Perching like small clay images.

Then with a noise of sudden rain
They clattered off again
And over Ballard Down
They circled like a flying town.

Though one could sooner blast a rock
Than scatter that dense flock
That through the winter weather
Some iron rule has held together,

Yet in another month from now
Love like a spark will blow
Those birds the country over
To drop in trees, lover by lover.

161. *Thistledown*

SILVER against blue sky
These ghosts of day float by,
Fitful, irregular,
Each one a silk-haired star,
Till from the wind's aid freed
They settle on their seed.

Not by the famished light
Of a moon-ridden night
But by clear sunny hours
Gaily these ghosts of flowers
With rise and swirl and fall
Dance to their burial.

INDEX OF FIRST LINES

INDEX OF FIRST LINES

INDEX OF FIRST LINES

INDEX OF FIRST LINES

INDEX OF FIRST LINES

INDEX OF FIRST LINES

INDEX OF FIRST LINES

THE END

Printed in Great Britain by R. & R. CLARK, LIMITED, *Edinburgh.*